MORE MEMORIES OF
BARNSLEY

The publishers would like to thank the following companies for their support in the production of this book

Main Sponsor
REXAM GLASS

Dale Products (Plastics) Ltd

Walter Frank & Sons Ltd

Hills Building Supplies Ltd

The Monckton Coke And Chemical Company Limited

Northern College for Residential Adult Education

C D Potter & Sons Ltd

Seals, Packing & Gaskets Ltd

Warwick Ward (Machinery) Ltd

First published in Great Britain by True North Books Limited
England HX3 6AE
01422 344344

ISBN 1 903204 79 8

Text, design and origination by True North Books Limited
Printed and bound by The Amadeus Press Limited

MORE MEMORIES OF
BARNSLEY

Contents

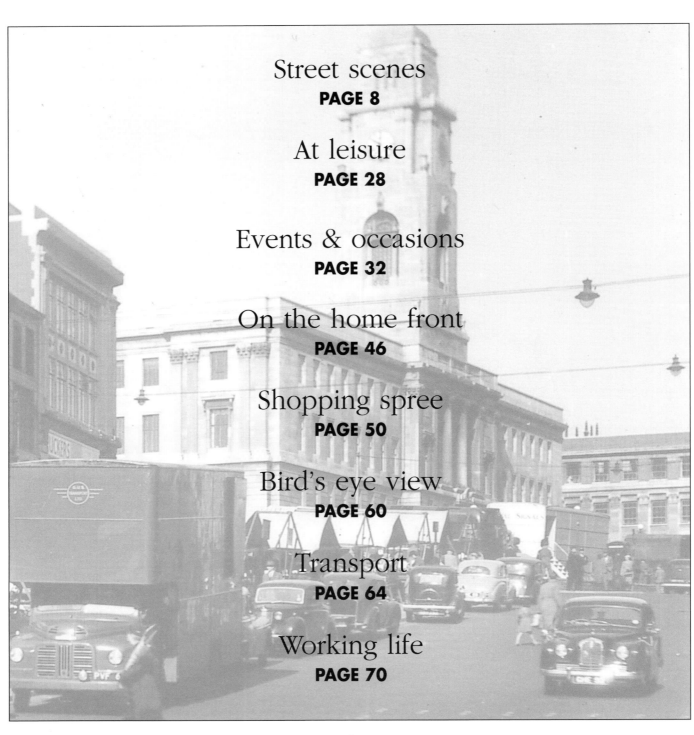

Street scenes
PAGE 8

At leisure
PAGE 28

Events & occasions
PAGE 32

On the home front
PAGE 46

Shopping spree
PAGE 50

Bird's eye view
PAGE 60

Transport
PAGE 64

Working life
PAGE 70

Introduction

Welcome to the world of 'More Memories of Barnsley'. It is a treasure trove of nostalgia, peeking back in time from the roaring 20s to the passing of the swinging 60s, providing readers with a flavour of our town as it has changed over that half century. As each page is turned we retrace our steps along such streets as Market Hill to catch a glimpse of the Butterfield and Massie family business where tea could be taken in genteel surroundings as shoppers took time out from the hurly burly of department store shopping. Further along we can shop again at Hart's, not far from the Town Hall, close to the pitched roofs of the market stalls. The book will assist us in saying a prayer once more at the Congregationalist Church on Regent Street or buying a sixpenny stamp at the old main Post Office. Elsewhere we can order some material from Jackson's furnishers on Peel Street or get a three piece suite on the never-never from Hardy and Co of Cheapside. All these journeys to buildings, businesses and streets that have been remodelled, renamed or simply disappeared are possible, thanks to the magic of the camera and a little imagination on behalf of the reader.

The images on the following pages show the changing face of the home town that we have come to love. Where once trams clanked along their tracks there are now pedestrianised ways. The redevelopment of the town centre shopping areas in the 1970s and the creation of new roads has meant that parts of Barnsley that are our heritage have been lost. Not only that, but the pace and style of life has altered dramatically from the days in which our grandparents held sway. How often have we wished that we could have spoken at more depth with them about the world they knew. Although we may have missed that opportunity, there is still the chance to gain some insight into an era when coinage was in the 'lsd' that referred to pounds, shillings and pence and not some form of hallucinatory drug, or when going on a trip meant a day out of town and not out of your head! All the photographs within have been enhanced by the attachment of captions intended to inform or even provoke comment. They are not image titles but text designed to highlight elements of each image and, at times, offer a pithy outlook on the background or times in which the scenes were observed. Hopefully, this will prompt the reader into reflecting on his or her own interpretation. Feel free to disagree, for then

we have succeeded in stimulating discussion. That can only be of benefit as we think back over how life might have been in the times depicted or how it really was if we are old enough to recall those days. Perhaps for some of us those memories have a hazy hue and the photographs will help bring everything flooding back. The camera never lies, though its angles might offer a slightly different perspective.

Barnsley is a town that must be among the most popular in Britain, if statistics are to be believed. One survey suggested that, on average, only 115 people relocate each year out of a borough that boasts a population of over 200,000. Many celebrities have hailed from this South Yorkshire town, but they all speak fondly of their roots, even if they have secured fame and fortune elsewhere. Arthur Scargill, the proud supporter of the miners and chief irritant to Margaret Thatcher, was born in Worsbrough Dale. Dickie Bird, the world renowned cricket umpire, lifted his first bat and, eventually his index finger, here. The poet and broadcaster Ian McMillan was born in Darfield and memories of actor and former wrestler Brian Glover in 'Kes' bring a smile to the face and a tear to the eye. Perhaps the best known face belongs to Michael Parkinson, the doyen of the TV chat show and sports feature writer supreme. Darren Gough, Mick McCarthy, Sam Nixon and many more will tell you that they are fiercely proud of their rich heritage.

Their origins are just part of the history that has seen Barnsley grow from a tiny settlement into the busy town it is today, with its construction, manufacturing, service and financial industries being especially strong. The first recorded reference can be found in William the Conqueror's Domesday Book with the citing of the existence of Crevesford and Berneslai, hamlets of no more than 200 souls. It is that latter name from which the modern spelling of Barnsley is derived. Saxon words of 'berne' and 'ley' meant 'barn' and 'field' respectively, obviously reflecting the rural nature of the district in those far off days. However, there are some who think that the name might have evolved from 'Beorn's ley', with the first word referring to an actual person. Soon after the Norman conquest of 1066, Barnsley, as we shall now continue to refer to the town, was given into the hands of the de Lace family who founded a priory in Pontefract. Henry III granted the town a charter in 1249, enabling it to hold markets and an annual fair. This paved the way for it to become a flourishing market town. Ownership passed from church hands to the Crown in 1539,

following Henry VIII's dissolution of the monasteries. Largely untroubled by the 17th century Civil War, Barnsley continued to gain importance. On the route of a main north-south coaching run to the capital, the town's inns and associated trades benefited handsomely. Coal mining, glass blowing and linen weaving all contributed to the economy, though they would have their pre-eminent days as the industrial revolution took hold in the second half of the 18th and throughout the 19th centuries. William Wilson introduced a small linen industry in 1744, with 500 domestic looms appearing in the town over the next 50 years. James Cocker's power loom, introduced in 1837, led to the first purpose built factory being established by Thomas Taylor in 1844. Within a decade there were mills dotted around Town End and, before long, fine goods were being exported across the globe.

Glass making was something of a traditional Barnsley craft. Bottles were manufactured in Gawber in the mid 18th century, though it would be in the following century that the industry truly took off. The Redfearn brothers' works at Old Mill and the Wood Brother Glass Company were two of the most prestigious of names from that era.

Coal, the industry with which most outsiders link Barnsley, was first mined in Saxon times, but became a major force from the late 1600s onwards. Huge deposits in the area provided large scale employment and the development of an integrated network of railways, canals and roads in Victorian times helped Barnsley to prosper. By the time the Queen's reign came to an end, the coal industry was the town's main employer. How times have changed, especially from the days before the decline of the 1970s and the miners' strike of the mid 1980s.

So, now let us return to 'More Memories of Barnsley' and allow ourselves to become nostalgia buffs as the waves of yesteryear wash over us. Why not embark on a chara ride to Cleethorpes instead of jetting off to the Maldives? Turn off the DVD player and switch on the wireless because it is time to listen to 'Journey into Space', 'ITMA' or 'The Goon Show'. Get out the starched petticoats and jitterbug to a Joe Loss band tune, but mind you do not turn an ankle when jiving to Danny and the Juniors' 'At the Hop' while wearing stiletto heels. Chew on a penny Arrow Bar, nibble on a Hirst's black pudding or go back to the nail biting days when the blackout curtains were drawn as we waited fearfully for the next siren to sound and it was off to the shelter. Turn the first page and, as modern waitresses annoyingly say, 'Enjoy'.

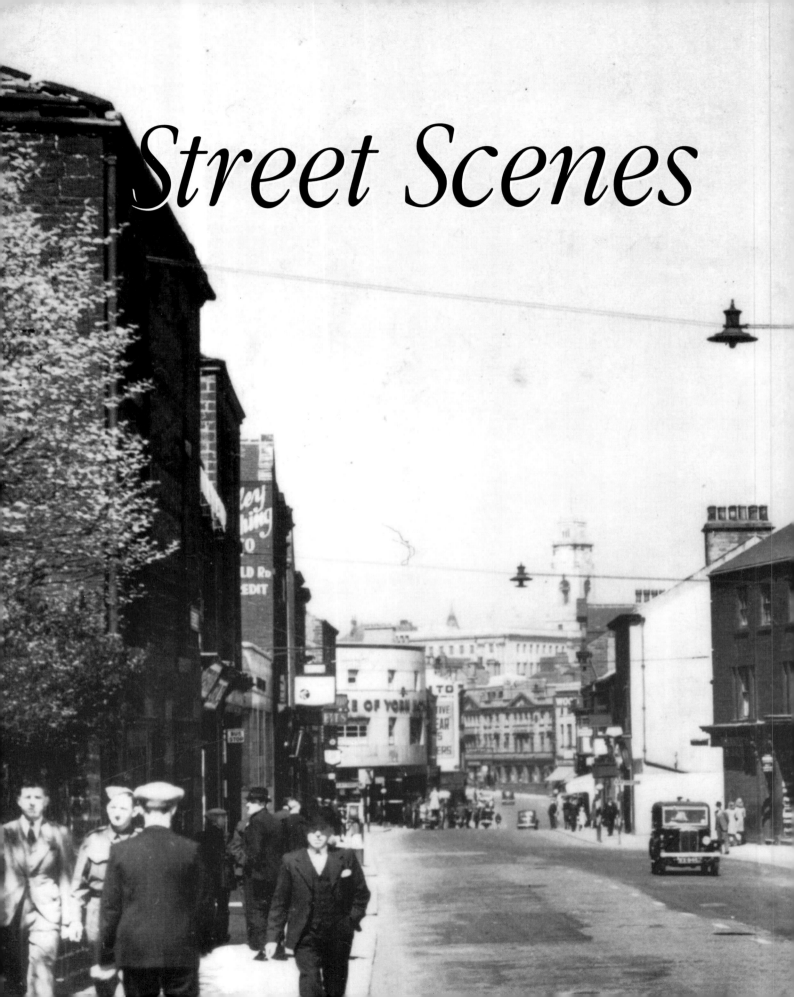

Street Scenes

Looking down towards the Duke of York at Cheapside, the building that takes the eye on Sheffield Road is the magnificent Alhambra. Such grandeur was typical of theatres and cinemas constructed by our forefathers. This building had begun life as a 2,600 seater theatre, being converted to a cinema in 1926. Those early reels would have brought such silent movies as 'Son of the Sheikh' to Barnsley. Its star, Rudolph Valentino, was to die in the very year that the Alhambra was converted, leading to much wailing and shedding of tears by star struck women who were besotted with his handsome looks. Men, not surprisingly, had more interest in Mary Pickford, 'America's sweetheart'. Older readers may recall their courting days after the second world war when they dodged the intrusive lights of the usherette's torches and cuddled up on the back row away from dad's prying eyes. Those were the days of double features, Tom and Jerry cartoons, Pathé news and a short travelogue, all for a shilling or two. On Saturday mornings youngsters enjoyed the humour of the Three Stooges and the cliff hanging drama of a Flash Gordon serial. The dreaded curse of bingo arrived in the early 1960s and the Alhambra became the Vale. This glorious piece of architectural heritage was lost when it was demolished in the late 1980s.

Pedestrians on Queen Street in the early interwar years had little traffic to worry them as they ambled across the carriageway. Cars were few and far between and you were just as likely to see a horse and cart as a vehicle fitted with an internal combustion engine. Of course, it is even safer these days as it is part of the pedestrianised area at the heart of Barnsley's shopping scene. The danger to life and limb is now more likely to come from some youth whizzing along on a scooter or skateboard. Barnsley Brewery's Three Cranes Hotel was closed down in October 1963, though by then it had been part of the John Smith's empire for two years. It opened in 1822 and was rebuilt in 1930, being

enlarged to include three neighbouring shops. London businessmen who had diverse commercial interests, of which beer was just one string to their bow, formed the Barnsley Brewery Company in 1888. The brewery had connections further back in time as it included the Oakwell Brewery in its acquisitions, a company founded by Paul and Guy Senior. The sons of Seth Senior, a Shepley brewer, they established their business at Beevor Hall, promoting Oakwell Ales as being 'as pure as the spring'. Barnsley Brewery quickly expanded in the latter years of the 19th century. By 1898 it had 93 tied houses. The growth continued into the following century, reaching 260 such outlets by the time of the 1961 takeover.

Below: Any visitor to Barnsley leaving Court House Station and heading up Regent Street was greeted with this delightful panorama, heightened by the sight of the War Memorial and splendour of the magnificent Town Hall. Who could fail to be impressed by the splendour of this municipal centre of local government? The Post Office towards the far end of the road and the other corner buildings were originally built with just two storeys, a third appearing at a later date. Stamps were first sold here in 1882 and the queues at the counter continued until 1967, though we hope that different people were standing in them by then! On the morning of 7 February 1950, R Needs & Company had offices for accountants and auditors to conduct their business on the corner with Royal Street. Eastgate is the road joining Regent Street just beyond the parked van. The County Court occupied the building opposite Needs' premises from 1871, having moved along the street from the building that became the station. Many of the offices along Regent Street were built as houses, but had long been redesignated by the business community. By 1950 the motor car was becoming a more frequent sight on our roads, though the days of widespread family motoring had not fully arrived. However, children no longer told their mums when a car came down their street as they had done before the war, excited by the novelty value.

Above: You needed your gloves and collar turned up against the chilly breeze blowing along Church Street at 12.15 pm on 11 January 1950. It was not just the bleak midwinter in terms of the weather, but a cold economic draught was still felt in Britain as the new decade got under way. Rationing was still with us, even though the war had ended over four years earlier. Britain devalued the pound by 30 per cent just a few months before this photograph was taken, sending tremors through the financial world. The cost of living rose by five per cent overnight and Sir Stafford Cripps, the Chancellor of the Exchequer, announced that he would put a stop to wage increases. He had spent a fortnight in secret talks with financial experts in Washington while his staff in London denied that there was any possibility of devaluation. Did you think that 'spin' was the invention of the modern Labour government? Think again; they were at it in the middle of the last century. No wonder these chaps tightened their topcoat belts as they approached the Mining and Technical College. This centre of excellence that opened in 1932 is somewhat overshadowed in architectural significance by the Town Hall, but its description as 'one of the best schools of learning' and 'the biggest mining college in the country' earned it an important standing. It now forms part of the multi-sited Barnsley College.

Above: Cooper Art Gallery stands on the east side of Church Street, just down from Barclays Bank. It was a sunny day in 1950 from the evidence of the shadows cast by the pedestrians. The gallery was built in 1660 when it was the Thomas Keresforth Grammar School. An inscription over the door reads 'Tout vient de Dieu' (everything comes from God). In 1886 it became the Holgate Grammar School, with accommodation on site for the headmaster who really did take his work home with him. In 1912 a local businessman and philanthropist, Samuel Joshua Cooper, bought the premises as a home for his own art collection. It was opened to the general public in 1914. The Fox family, local brewers and hoteliers, donated an extra wing and a collection of oils. During the second world war the paintings were dispersed when the gallery was requisitioned as an annexe to Beckett's Hospital and the gallery did not reopen to the public until 1957. It underwent major refurbishment at the start of this century, reopening its doors in May 2001. Barnsley MBC took over the administration of the building on behalf of the Cooper Trustees in 1986. Today, the gallery tries to promote the work of contemporary, local artists as well as providing a showcase for national touring exhibitions.

Below: The cars driving along Regent Street were heading down towards the bus coming under the Court House Station bridge, demolished in 1961. The morning of 20 January 1950 was long before two way traffic was banned in the attempt to free the congestion in and around the Town Hall by the introduction of a one way system, coupled with the road improvement scheme at the bottom of town. The woman making her way across the pedestrian crossing used the road studs to guide her over. The alternating black and white rectangles that gave birth to the zebra crossing nickname were still a couple of years into the future. Belisha beacons and pedestrian crossings came to us before the war. Britain's record of road safety was appalling and the measures brought in during the mid 1930s that included Percy Shaw's cats' eyes, Belisha beacons, the Highway Code, compulsory driving tests and the spread of electrically controlled traffic lights all helped to improve our track record. The Shell oil tanker, turning from Church Street, was owned by the company that ran a series of jolly TV adverts in the 1960s and 1970s. It was one of the firms that recognised the value of catchy slogans, with 'Keep going well, keep going Shell' being one of the most memorable. Musical jingles helped reinforce the company's name in our minds and even inspired a number one hit record for Georgie Fame with 'Get away' in 1966.

Above: The couple on the left wore warm ankle boots to keep out the icy chill. Their headscarves were as much a sign of modesty as an attempt to keep warm. Not many women were daring enough to go out into town without some form of headwear. Only common folk did that and these two were ladies. It was 11 am on 21 January 1950 and we did not have global warming to make our winters mild. Jack Frost knew when to come nipping and we had some horrendous weather to contend with at times. These women remembered the big freeze of three years earlier when blizzards swept the country just as a fuel crisis hit Britain. The RAF dropped food parcels to isolated hamlets and everyone shivered by candlelight as power cuts hit our homes. In recent years January has often been a wet month, but in the middle of the last century there was every chance that the kids could go sliding down snowy slopes on tin trays. When was the last time you saw a snowman in the garden? Our climate really has altered. The couple was looking across Church Street at Gordon Charlesworth's tobacconist's shop. He traded there 1933-55, following a line of similar retailers that included E Burnett (1888-95) and LA Shaw (1896-1932). E Banks succeeded Charlesworth in 1955. Further along the row were Smith and Iberson, solicitors, Hobson's sweets, Rideal and Sons, solicitors, and the Royal Insurance Company offices.

Right: We cannot tell you how many Barnsley workmen it takes to change a light bulb, but it obviously requires at least six to erect a lamp standard. There is one, out of shot, to operate the crane, two to guide the post and three to stand around and watch. That seems about right for any council job. The highways department workforce always seemed to have a 50 per cent deployment of observers whenever the roads were dug up, so it was only in keeping for the men erecting the first concrete lampposts in the borough to follow the same practice. Come to think of it, things have not changed that much in the intervening years. How often have we driven past roadworks or along a stretch of the M1 that is coned off and wondered where the workforce had got to? We would give thanks if we saw half of the people gainfully employed instead of the more usual scene of complete isolation. This work was taking place on Market Hill, just below Shambles Street, in 1954. It seems strange to think now that concrete encased electric lights were something of a novelty half a century ago. What will future generations take for granted that we, in the early years of the new millennium, regard as innovative ventures?

Above: Victorians loved to name their hostelries and streets after famous figures and events that had significance in underlining the strength of the British Empire. The Lord Nelson and the Lord Clive are pubs that can be found in many towns, as are Gordon Street, Balaclava Terrace and Albert Road. The Wellington Hotel belonged to that same group. It had started life as the Lamb Inn, presumably echoing some of the rural and market life in and around Barnsley, in 1825. It was rebuilt and renamed in 1867, taking the title of the duke who was born Arthur Wellesley in 1769. As the Duke of Wellington, the hero of the Waterloo victory over Napoleon's forces served his country as its prime minister (1828-30). The pub that bore his name was demolished not long after this photograph was taken in 1962. It was the beginning of the end for many of the older buildings that the town planners decided had run their course as they looked to modernise Barnsley. As the Wellington's cellars fell dry, momentous events were taking place in the skies above. John Glenn became the first American to orbit the earth when his Mercury capsule performed three circuits of the globe. The gauntlet had now been thrown down to the Russians in the race for the ultimate prize, the landing of a man on the moon. If he had been a Victorian Englishman we would be supping in the Glenn Arms today.

Top right: The road marking was good advice to motorists in 1959 as they headed along Church Street. There was a hidden junction with Regent Street to the left that sometimes caught out the careless trying to make a quick turn. It was also advisable to take it easy down the slope as they entered the stretch of the road that became Market Hill beyond Shambles Street. The buildings down the left hand side include Barclays Bank in the foreground, the Royal Hotel in the centre and Butterfields and Massies just beyond. To the right we can see the Halifax Building Society and the war memorial nearer to the camera. This structure stands close to the gardens now dedicated to the memory of Diana, Princess of Wales who was killed in a car crash in Paris in the late summer of 1997. The war memorial was officially unveiled in 1925. Large crowds

attended the ceremony held in honour of those who made the ultimate sacrifice during World War I. Men doffed their caps and bowed their heads in remembrance of those who would never return and the women shed tears openly for the loved ones they had lost. They included the volunteers known as the Barnsley Pals, members of the 13th and 14th Battalions of the York and Lancaster Regiment that sustained heavy losses, particularly on the Somme in 1916. Pals' regiments were commonplace during this war when friends, neighbours and workmates were enlisted together. The idea was to foster team spirit, but for the unlucky ones, this meant that whole communities were decimated. It was a practice that the Army never repeated.

Right: This was Pontefract Road at the junction with Sheffield Road before the property in this area was gutted and the streets remodelled to provide the system around West Way and Harborough Hill Road that we have today. Younger

readers may puzzle over the '10 gns' sign in the electrical goods shop. The abbreviation stood for 'guineas' that, even by the 1960s, was an archaic term. The guinea was an English gold coin issued from 1663 to 1813 and fixed in 1717 at 21 shillings (£1.05). In typically idiosyncratic fashion, Britain continued to use the word even though no corresponding coin existed. The 10 guineas being charged for a factory rebuilt cleaner meant that the price was £10 10s (£10.50). The cleaner was not some reconditioned, robotic Mrs Mopp but a Hoover or its equivalent. A customer who did not have the cash could get the aid to domestic bliss on 'easy terms' or 'tick', as we used to call credit. The shop was so confident in its machines that it allowed housewives to have a free home trial and offered a 12 month guarantee. The Duke of York Hotel at 29 Cheapside opened in 1822. The Bookers were well known figures in the pub's history in the early 20th century. Harry was the landlord and George provided the charabancs for hotel outings. It closed in 1966.

Below: The stalls of the fish market, to the right under the hoarding, are no more. Sadly, neither is the Cross Keys Hotel. Erected originally in 1825, it was rebuilt 40 years later and was part of Barnsley's heritage until February 1972. Drinking in the Cross Keys was a touch different from most of the other hostelries in the town as the aroma of fresh fish blended with the hops and malt of Barnsley bitter. Apart from that, however, the experience was much the same in that beer was supped from pint pots by men who recalled watching Tommy Taylor bang in goals at Oakwell before becoming a Busby Babe and achieving sad immortality at Munich in 1958. Others drooled over the silky skills of Danny Blanchflower before he found fame with Aston Villa and Spurs. The drinkers at the bar would not have appreciated conversation about pop idols, hair gel or designer gear. Nor would they have thought much about the modern trend of quaffing prettily coloured liquid straight from the bottle while attempting to press buttons on a mobile phone to send someone a message. Pubs were where you supped rather than yapped, except if Arthur Kaye was mentioned. Now there was a forward with some power in his boots, and did any of you ever see anyone head a ball as well as Gordon Pallister? Another? Don't mind if I do.

Right: This is Sheffield Road, as seen from the Cemetery Road junction in 1968. The Coach and Horses, built in 1825, was part of the Barnsley Brewery empire. The snack bar on the right was home to the Star Libraries until 1958

and became WA Wike's greengrocer's in 1973. About this time all the individual food shops would start to feel the pinch as the popularity of supermarkets began to make a major impression on trade. With their pile 'em high sell 'em cheap philosophy, supermarkets soon drove many a poor shopkeeper to the wall, unable to compete with the variety on offer at bargain prices in the self service world. Many young children today do not realise that we once had a seasonal nature to our diets. Sprouts were a wintertime vegetable and peas appeared in the summer. Fresh fruit was plentiful when the sun shone, whereas we relied on imported bananas later in the year. Now, of course, these products are on our shelves all the year round. Youngsters living in large towns may never have been into a butcher's, a dairy or a baker's as meat, milk and bread comes ready packaged and stacked neatly along the aisles. One child we know was asked in a test at school if he knew where bacon came from. He replied 'Tesco's'.

Top right: Viewed from Church Street, the road improvements at Old Mill Lane Top were well under way in July 1965. There was little traffic to be seen, though this was unusual at this major intersection. Even so, the volume of cars on the roads pales in comparison to the large headaches we have today attempting to cope with our rush hour jams and snarl-ups.

The road from Huddersfield is a nightmare for those attempting to get into town in the morning. But, even 40 years ago, Barnsley was experiencing the first, dubious fruits of the boom years. The austerity of much of the previous decade had gone, replaced by a growth in consumerism as jobs and money were in plentiful supply. Homes boasted the best of everything electrical. Washing machines, tumble driers, fridges, televisions and radiograms became necessities and not luxuries. The vast majority of families also had a car. The family saloon became a familiar sight on driveways and at the kerbs outside houses that had been built long before people had the inclination, cash or space to erect garages. In the late 1960s and early 1970s roads in and around every town centre were widened or completely remodelled. New ring roads appeared. Despite heavy investment, we failed to cope with the ever greater number of vehicles that demanded space on our thorough-fares and, even now, the problem persists.

Above: Barnsley may not be the biggest town in the country but its town hall ranks up there with the best. Shops and houses along part of the west side of Church Street were demolished in the late 1920s as part of a slum clearance programme that helped pave the way for a new seat of local government and the neighbouring Mining and Technical College, just seen beyond the town hall. Viewed from Market Hill, the grand edifice rose above the foundation stone laid by Mayor Jonas Plummer on 21 April 1932. The Prince of Wales performed the official opening ceremony, using a golden key, on Thursday, 14 December 1933. The building was criticised by some for its cost. One of its most notable critics included the author George Orwell who, in 'Road to Wigan Pier', made reference to public expenditure in a time of public need. In defence of those who approved its building, it must be pointed out that the creation of the town hall and college provided employment for construction workers in a time of depression and want. The town received its armorial bearing in 1869 and a bust of the first mayor, Henry Richardson, stands in the foyer today. Barnsley achieved county borough status in 1913. We can be rightly proud of our town hall as its grandeur is something to be cherished and not sniffed at by members of the landless gentry, as Orwell might have described himself.

Below: Seen from the corner of Waltham Street, Sheffield Road runs northwest towards what is now the roundabout at the back of the Alhambra shopping centre. Union Court and Union Street are to the left, with Taylor Row off to the right. R Oxtaby and Son had the shop at No 117, first supplying local shoppers with their meagre rations in 1943. It continued in business here until 1968, five years after this photograph was taken. Oxtaby's referred to itself as a 'high class butcher'. That has always been something of a meaningless description used by countless similar outlets up and down the country. Who would say that he was a low class butcher? Further along we can see the traditional red and white stripe of the barber's pole at No 113. Mason's hairdresser's had been here since 1903. Further along, RF Walker's ladies outfitters occupied several adjacent shop fronts. How different the fashions were in 1936 when the first customers came in through the door. The pubs on either side of the street, the Rising Sun and the Spotted Leopard, at the time were kept by Mary Wood and Frank Mawer, respectively. He had just taken over the Spotted Leopard from the Mills family who had held the licence for 50 years. The Rising Sun opened in 1862 and was enlarged in 1898 when the house next door was incorporated. Its rival served its first pint in 1868.

Above: Dilapidated, run down and truly living up to the street's name by the time that 1964 came along, these shops were an eyesore on Shambles Street. Later that year they were demolished and eventually replaced by a new parade of modern shops that included British Relay, Peter Watson's tobacconists and Les White's menswear outlet. The last businesses in these former premises at 20-24 Shambles Street belonged to Green's Radio, Don Valley Cleaners and N Robinson, a locksmith. The radio shop had branched out into the world of television, as it had to in order to survive as entertainment in the home changed in the late 1950s. At the start of that decade there were few homes that could afford the sets that were dismissively referred to as 'goggle boxes'. There was just one channel, run by the BBC. Interest in the new form of broadcasting was kindled by the national coverage of the Queen's coronation in 1953. When ITV was launched in September 1955, with programmes aimed at a more populist audience, the future of television was guaranteed. By the time that Green's Radio closed down, only the snooty refused to have a TV in the corner of the living room. Pictures were still in black and white, but that did not reduce the enjoyment of watching such classics as 'The Avengers' with Patrick McNee and Diana Rigg.

Below: Grange Lane, looking south from Abbey Lane at Cundy Cross, was awash yet again in 1970. The River Dearne was in flood, not an uncommon experience. Although river defences, using flood banks and weirs to control the water flow have been introduced over the years, the low lying land is still prone to flash flooding because of the rapid runoff upstream after heavy rains. Although the level soon falls back to normal, the effect on the lives of householders unlucky enough to have had the water enter their homes merits sympathy. The Dearne rises east of Huddersfield and flows through Barnsley before joining the River Don at Conisborough. Although a mere trickle in comparison with major watercourses, the Dearne has had an impact on Barnsley life for many years, and not just when it is in spate. In the 18th century the town was poorly served by roads and the developing coalmining industry had difficulty in moving its output quickly and in volume. In 1792 the Don Navigation Company determined that it would make the Dearne navigable from the Don up to Barnsley. Eventually, changed plans were adopted that saw the construction of the newly named Dearne and Dove Canal begin in an exercise that would take 11 years to complete the waterway from Swinton to the junction with Barnsley Canal.

Bretton's driving school on Regent Street South had a number of cancelled lessons in the winter of 1964 when the snow lay on the ground. This was a pity as learner drivers would have done well to experience at first hand tricky driving conditions while they had the benefit of an experienced instructor alongside them. The driving test was not introduced until the mid 1930s, but it was not until the wider public embraced private motoring that driving schools came to play a part in promoting good driving habits, Before their popularity it was left up to a family member to risk life and limb, not to mention his prized motor car, in teaching a learner driver how to become a knight of the road. Driving tests were a little different from the sort we have now. There was no written test. Everything was left to performance behind the wheel on the day. The examination began with an eyesight test with a candidate being asked to read a number plate on a car parked nearby. Those with Mr Magoo vision memorised possible ones close to the test centre before entering the building. After a 20 minute drive, the learner was asked a few simple questions from the Highway Code. One other difference from today's style of testing is that you used to be required to use hand signals and not just electric indicators. In this photograph we are looking at the entrance to the yard that contained workshops and warehouses that extended to the side of the Harvey Institute.

In 1969 the photographer was perched high on the tower of the Town Hall to get this elevated view to the northwest across Churchfield. To do his job required more than just film and a camera, a head for heights was definitely something to be recommended. The old cottages that were in this area had been swept away a few years earlier. Leafy Churchfield runs west from the rear of St Mary's Church, a building that has its origins in the 12th century, though most of the present structure dates from 1821. The turret on the left belongs to the court house. It had been in use since 1879 when new cells were also built behind the Police Superinten-dent's house. These cells made it possible for the prisoners to be taken straight into court without being seen by the public. In the 1970s, a new Magistrates' Court was built on Church Fields and is still in use after recent alterations. A new police station was built in the 1960s. Quarter sessions were held in Barnsley during the 14th century in the Old Moot Hall in Market Place. This building served the town until 1794 when, because of the hall's poor state of repair, the courts were moved to a part of a former workhouse near to the site of the present town hall. A new police station, court and town hall opened in 1834.

Right: The advertising of cigarettes on television was banned in 1965. Critics of the announcement made in the House of Commons by the Minister of Health, Kenneth Robinson, said that discrimination between the various media was illogical. Television programmes began in the evening, but newspaper adverts and roadside hoardings could appear all day long. Manufacturers were also allowed to continue to distribute coupons to young people offering them free cigarettes. The arguments fell on deaf ears and the tobacco giants sought to find alternatives to television in their push to gather more addicts into their nets. Smoking was made to appear one of life's bits of fun and attractive models were used to add glamour to even the most ordinary of cigarettes, as in this Park Drive advert. The Americans continued to promote their Marlborough with an actor portraying a clean living cowboy, but got a shock in recent years when he contracted cancer. This photograph was taken in 1967 and shows the abutments of Eldon Street bridge and the entrance to the goods yard at Court House Station. The station opened in the building that had been built as the town's Court House in 1861, but was transformed in May 1870. It closed in 1960, but was refurbished by Wetherspoon's and reopened as a bar in April 1999. It is a Grade II listed building.

Below: Close to where the Transport Interchange now stands, this kiosk on the corner of Midland Street was well placed to do a brisk passing trade in the 1950s. Although Wall's ice cream was dispensed over the little counter, it was the cigarettes on sale that brought in the most business. This was a time when smoking was a manly thing to do or something smart and a little daring if you were one of the fairer sex. Although Woodbines and Park Drive had been referred to as 'coffin nails' for many years, some other brands were promoted in a way that made them sound beneficial. Craven A even had a slogan that urged you to smoke them 'for your throat's sake' and Consulate were 'as cool as a mountain stream'. It was not until the mid 1960s that television adverts were withdrawn, leaving us with the 'you're never alone with a Strand' message as the last of its type. By then, some tobacco companies had moved into the realms of promoting their products with hints that their cigarettes would change your life and make you more socially or sexually attractive. Others tried humour to encourage consumers to light up, as in a series of Hamlet cigar adverts based in sand bunkers and photograph booths.

It was the day of the Crane Moor Working Men's Club outing in the summer of 1935. Such a special occasion was eagerly anticipated for weeks before. We have become rather blasé about jetting off to foreign climes a couple of times each year or popping off to the coast or to a theme park whenever the fancy takes us. It was a different story in the depression years. Unemployment was high and wages were low. Just a year after this photograph was taken men from the Jarrow shipyards marched on London to protest about their plight. Fancy holidays were few and far between. A day trip from Crane Moor

At leisure

to Cleethorpes or Bridlington was a treat to be talked about for weeks to come. Most of the children on the front row will be well into their 70s by now. Perhaps they can remember which place was to be the destination for their 'chara'. It must amuse younger readers to see the two older lads pointing their bare knees at the camera, but boys did not wear long trousers until they were bursting out of short ones. Many schools, even into the 1960s, had a regulation that enforced short trousers as mandatory uniform until boys were about 13. It did not matter if they were five feet or six feet tall at that age. Rules were rules!

Below: 'Be prepared' and this trio of Pitt Street guiders must have been for they clutched their certificates with pride. We do not know the award, but the Girl Guide Association provided the opportunity of following a variety of interests. Badges and certificates were on offer for those who displayed a proficiency in woodcraft, cookery, road safety, self-sufficiency, music, art etc. Most guides graduated from being brownies, the junior section established in 1914. Just listening to those names and looking at these happy girls conjures up images of rosebuds, pixies, and elves in the magical fairy world that Enid Blyton created. They were the days when childhood was something special in its own right and not just a transitional phase into adulthood. As the last century reached its latter stages, being a guide or becoming a brownie began to slip in popularity. Attempts were made to modernise the Association and rekindle its attraction. In 1990 the designer, Jeff Banks, was commissioned to update the traditional uniform, though the range of brownie baseball caps he included did not meet with universal approval. A new wording for the Promise was introduced in 1993 and, the following year, the word 'girl' was dropped from the Association name. That title did not last long and the Guide Association became Girlguiding UK in 2002. But, what's in a name? Surely the importance of the organisation can be measured from the sheer delight and pride on the faces of these happy lasses. Let us hope that their daughters, 35 years later, have shared the same experiences.

Below: Reverend A Bradford stood alongside the Pitt Street Methodist Church's girl guides in a scene posed in the late 1960s. Notice that even these youngsters had some thought of fashion in the way they wore the skirts of their uniforms. They had hitched them up high in the style favoured by mini skirt designer Mary Quant. Secondary school headmistresses went berserk during this period of history in attempting to enforce school policy as hemlines became more like pelmets. They tried to enforce the regulations by making girls kneel down in order to check that their skirts touched the floor. Once the old dragons' backs were turned they just yanked them back up again as high as modesty or detection would allow. These Pitt Street girls were proud of their uniforms and what they stood for, but that did not mean they had to look dowdy. These guides followed a long line of tradition that went back to the early days of the 20th century when Agnes Baden-Powell (1858-1945) decided to match her brother Robert's example. He founded the Boy Scout movement in 1907 after running a trial camp on Brownsea Island near Poole in Dorset. Everything seemed to be run for male benefit back then, as the suffragettes would testify. Agnes decided to do something about the imbalance and the Girl Guides were born in 1910.

Events & occasions

Barnsley has had its fair share of royal visitors over the years. On 12 July 1912 King George V, accompanied by Queen Mary, was in town. It was a very different world from the one we know today, nearly 100 years on. Just as the King was visiting Barnsley a second reading of the Franchise Bill was being heard in the House of Commons. This was in the early days of movement towards granting women the right to vote, but they should not have got their hopes up. The bill was abandoned the following January, leading to an outcry from suffragists and inspiring hunger strikes, the bombing of Lloyd George's golf villa and the implementation of Asquith's 'cat and mouse' strategy

of arrest, release and immediate re-arrest. Women would only get partial suffrage after the first world war and had to wait until 1928 for full voting rights. When the King visited our town he had only been on the throne for just over two years. His consort, who became famous for wearing heavily decorated hats and colourful toques, had been engaged to George's elder brother, Albert, but he died a few weeks before their wedding was due to take place. Mary of Teck, as she then was, married the future king in 1893. Despite her Germanic background, her concern with the welfare of servicemen in World Wars I and II helped to make her popular with all classes of the British people.

All these children were born during the latter stages of World War I. What a difficult start to life many of them must have had. Their fathers were away at the front when they were in nappies, leaving the mums to struggle on trying to make ends meet and raising the family single-handedly. Sadly for some of them that situation was to be their lot for evermore, should their husbands be among the millions who fell during the most fearful hostilities the world had ever seen. The men who made it back had to try to rebuild their lives and bond with children who were almost strangers to them. The little ones also had to adjust to the stranger in their midst. The children at Crane Moor Infants look to have been a well balanced bunch of normal kiddies, if this photograph from 1922 is any evidence. They had obviously put on their best clothes for this class record. Little girls with bows in their hair and lads in sailor suits and wide collars posed with their teacher as children have done in schools all over Britain ever since. Trends in education may change, but the annual class photograph lives on. Sadly, some of these earnest faces failed to make it through the next world war, but the handful who might still be around today will still have fond memories of the chalk and talk days spent at Crane Moor Infants.

Crane Moor
Infants
W62 1922

This was, with little doubt, the society wedding of the year at All Saints, Darton's parish church. On 27 August 1921 Sir William Sutherland (1880-1949) and Miss Annie Christine Fountain (1874-1949) were married in a ceremony that was attended by local and national dignitaries, as well as the usual friends and family members. Although neither could hardly be said to be in the first flush of youth, their happiness was apparent to everyone in the congregation. Sutherland had been created a KCB in 1918, mainly in recognition of his service to the country during World War I. As a Member of Parliament, he rose

through the ranks to become David Lloyd George's private secretary, filling several positions at the Treasury, Ministry of munitions and the War Office. He became the Junior Lord of the Treasury in 1919, was the Chancellor of the Duchy of Lancaster in 1921 and became a privy councillor the following year. Christine, as she was usually known, had a similarly distinguished background. The daughter of Joseph and Catherine Fountain, she was brought up in wealthy surroundings. Her family were pit owners and made Birthwaite Hall their home. There are several windows in the parish church dedicated to the Fountains. This happy couple made their

home at the Hall and, after Lady Sutherland inherited the Fountain and Burnley mines, her husband acted as her manager. His name lives on in the Scottish shinty cup competition he inaugurated in 1923. Some of the other guests at the wedding in Darton Parish Church lifted their hats in respect as David Lloyd George and his wife walked under the good luck arbour and down the path. This couple was one of the more prestigious attending the ceremony and merited more than a second glance. He was born in 1863 in Manchester, the son of a Pembrokeshire headmaster. Lloyd George was just a baby when his father died, leaving the family in dire financial straits. They moved back to Wales, relying on support from his mother's brother, a Baptist minister from whom the young David drew for inspiration in his formative years. As a young

man he was notorious for his involvement in a number of love affairs, something that hardly changed even after his marriage to Margaret Owen in 1888. Had the tabloid press of today been around a century ago his career might have been blighted by his frequent acts of infidelity. However, in his day such behaviour did not reach the ears of the general public. Lloyd George entered Parliament in 1890, winning the Caernarvon Boroughs seat that he was to hold for the Liberals for 55 years. He rose steadily through the political ranks to serve as Prime Minister (1916-22). Lloyd George possessed eloquence, extraordinary charm and persuasiveness. He had a profound sympathy with oppressed classes and races and a genuine hatred of those who abused power, but he could also be devious and ruthless. He was raised to the peerage not long before his death in 1945.

Above: Scout Dike Reservoir has a capacity of 156 million gallons and covers a surface area of about 35 acres. The dam stands 40 feet high. Situated in a triangle with Royd Moor and Ingbirchworth reservoirs, Scout Dike has become popular with bird watchers and lovers of wildlife. Situated to the north of Penistone, just off the A629 that links Rotherham and Huddersfield, it is a popular starting point for ramblers exploring the northern edges of the Peak District. It was opened in 1928. Work began on 22 May 1924 with this gathering that brought together local worthies keen to lend their moral support. The church was also represented, ensuring divine inspiration could be added to the efforts of mere mortals in digging out the tons of earth over the next four years. The construction of the reservoir provided employment for men in the locality who had found, to their cost, that the end of the Great War had not brought a conclusion to the country's economic problems. Ramsay MacDonald, Labour's first Prime Minister, had highlighted housing and unemployment as major government issues, but identification and solution are different animals. Among the VIPs in attendance was Mayor CF Wood, looking very smart in his chain of office, made for £200 in 1871 by Garrard's of London. A future mayor in Councillor Cassells stood behind Councillor Wood as they listened to the address being given by Alderman Raley, chairman of the Water Committee.

Below: As the population increased and existing services became overburdened it was necessary to upgrade many of our established facilities. The reliable provision of good quality water in plentiful supply was just one of the ventures that local and national government had to give attention to. After the Great War there was a need to provide better housing that gave an improved standard of living. Many Victorian homes lacked many of the things that we now take for granted, such as running water, decent sanitary arrangements and an end to overcrowding, so creating an environment in which children could grow up without a fear of disease. As part of this drive to give Britons a better future, new reservoirs were created. Here, Mayor GF Wood was cutting the first sod in what was to become Scout Dike Reservoir. Surrounded by various town hall officers and elected members, plus an assorted array of other VIPs, he ceremonially lifted the first piece of earth in a project that was to take four years to complete. On 22 May 1924 even the act of digging just a single turf had to be observed according to the social structure of the day. The mayor had his robes and chain of office and so held centre stage. In the front row of those watching were the bewigged legal fraternity and bowler hatted middle class. Behind them stood those in homburgs and trilbies, while the poor souls who could only aspire to flat caps occupied the next rank. Women, of course, stood there as well.

Right: It all began in 1844 in a little shop on Toad Lane, Rochdale and a group calling itself the Equitable Society of Pioneers. The society created a set of organisational and working rules that have been widely adopted. They included open membership, democratic control, no religious or political discrimination, sales at prevailing market prices and the setting aside of some earnings for education. The co-operative movement, as it became known, soon spread to the rest of Britain. By 1861, the message had reached Barnsley. Later to become known as the 'nine men of vision', a group held a meeting in a temperance hotel on May Day Green. They had just nine shillings (45p) to put into the kitty. They agreed to contribute a small weekly amount and follow the philosophy as laid down by the Rochdale men. Within a month they had £3 5s (£3.25) and by the year end had attracted 68 members. The Barnsley British Co-operative Society was off and running. The first shop was opened on Market Street four years later. In 1935 the foundation stone for the branch at Yews Lane, Worsbrough Dale was laid by Captain Alfred E Allott JP, the Society's vice president. We can make an educated guess at the amount of cement he really put on his trowel by looking at his pristine, white shirt.

Below: The bobby in the background seems highly amused that it is taking three men to cut one ceremonial tape, and with some difficulty as well. It was hardly the most taxing of duties, but perhaps this trio was more used to pushing a pen than operating such complicated machinery as a pair of scissors! This was the occasion of the opening of Griffiths Bridge at Royston on 20 June 1934. Coincidentally, London's old Waterloo Bridge was being dismantled at the same time as this ribbon was finally severed. The bridge spanned Barnsley Canal, the waterway that was created over 200 years ago in order to provide cheap transport for the coal being mined from the rich veins in the coalfields northwest of the town around Silkstone. In June 1793, after much wrangling with the Don Navigation and Calder and Hebble companies, an act of Parliament was passed that permitted the Aire and Calder company to develop the canal. On 27 September of that year work began on building 16 miles of waterway, cut to a depth of 5 feet. The work was overseen by the eminent William Jessop, the engineer also responsible for the prestigious Grand Junction and Rochdale canals. The first section was opened in 1799, though the full project took several more years to complete. Barnsley Canal cost £95,000 to construct, but its value to the coal industry was immense. Although the 19th century was the period when it was particularly useful, there were still nearly 200,000 tons of coal being transported on the canal in 1914. The last boat passed under Royston Bridge in 1950.

Through the past clearly

The first man-made glass was probably produced by accident around 3,000 years BC when merchants delivering natron crude soda used some of it to prop up their cooking pots on sandy soil. The soda melted into the sand creating a new and remarkable substance. Glass can be made simply by melting silica such as sand, flint and quartz, but it requires very high temperatures to do so; the addition of soda or potash brings that temperature down to around a 'mere' 1,600 degrees Celsius.

It was not however, until the first century BC that a Syrian glassworker founded the modern glass industry by blowing into a tube connected to a lump of molten glass.

Since then the demand for glass has been insatiable, and its production has become a major industry - and nowhere more so than in Barnsley.

Rexam Glass, Monk Bretton, Barnsley, is part of Rexam plc, one of the world's top five consumer packaging groups. The headquarters of the group are in London but its operations are global in scale. The group supplies packaging solutions to the beauty, food, beverage, consumer and pharmaceutical industries in a variety of materials.

Top: Where it all started, Redfearn Brothers Limited, Old Glass Mill Bottle Works, Barnsley. Below: A late 19th century photograph of Redfearn workers.

It was in 1892 that two brothers Joshua and Samuel Redfearn founded a glass business 'Redfearn Brothers' at a factory which later became known as 'The Old Mill Factory' situated in Harborough Hills Road, Barnsley. In fact the Redfearn brothers actually bought an existing business which had been established even earlier by the side of the Barnsley Canal near the town's old corn mill by one John Wragg. Wragg went on to a new and anonymous career as a local pork butcher; the Redfearn brothers went on to fame and fortune.

Soon four furnaces were in production, with 30 'working holes' each manned by a team of five making glass by hand producing half pint bottles at a rate of eight gross in a ten and a half hour shift.

Across the world the Rexam Group employs some 21,000 people in 20 countries and has an annual turnover of more than £3 billion. Rexam is made up of a number of clearly defined manufacturing sectors, Beverage Can (Americas), Beverage Can (Europe & Asia), Beauty and Pharma, Plastic Containers and of course, Glass.

And it's glass which brings us back to Barnsley. The Rexam name first appeared in Barnsley in 1999 when the group put in a successful bid of £396 million for one of Barnsley's oldest manufacturers, then known as PLM Redfearn.

Joshua Redfearn died in 1897, his brother Samuel in 1900. Their estate was divided between their nephew Harry Redfearn, Harry Sykes Jessop and William Asquith. The business became a private limited company, Redfearn Brothers Ltd, in 1910.

By the outbreak of the first world war in 1914

Top and above: *Early 20th century views inside Redfearn Glass Mill Bottle Works.* ***Right:*** *Bottle making.*

the firm had a workforce of 600 and its engineering and commercial skills were widely acclaimed.

During the war two of William Asquith's sons served as lieutenants with local regiments, and both were gassed. Milton Asquith's batman was a Redfearn employee who despite losing a leg resumed his duty with the firm after the war; others were not so lucky, four other employees never returned.

Though women were employed during the war as packers and checkers the labour shortage created a new need for mechanisation. In 1915 the first 'Owens' machine with six arms was installed.

William Asquith was succeeded by his son Harry on his death in 1926.

By 1935 the business employed 750 workers and had five furnaces and 18 fully automatic machines in operation. The machines were run 24 hours a day with men working six shifts and then resting for two days. Some 50 million bottles a year were now being produced in all shapes and sizes at a rate of 27 per minute. This involved the annual consumption of 20,000 tons of Belgian sand and 7,000 tons of soda bicarbonate. The factory also burned 14,000 tons of coal to produce gas to fire the furnace.

In the United Kingdom milk bottles were the single biggest product line, whilst abroad beer and whisky bottles were made for the USA, by now happily having washed its hands of its experiment with prohibition.

The outbreak of the second world war in 1939 led to new labour shortages, and to shortages of materials, whilst the increased demand for substitutes for steel led to a demand for light weight glass containers.

Inspired by Milton Asquith, who had become Managing Director on the

Top: Management and staff pose for a group photograph. Far left: The Machin Glass Bottle machine which had an average capacity of 600 bottles per hour. Left: One of the company's first bottle making machines.

from Redfearn Brothers became Chairman, whilst John LC Pratt, William Pratt's son became Vice Chairman and Stanley Race became Managing Director.

The new company now began planning for the future and in 1968 No 7 furnace was built at Monk Bretton. The new furnace was then the largest in the United Kingdom with a theoretical melting capacity of 450 tonnes; this led, later that same year, to the closure of the Old Mill factory.

Led by Stanley Race the business entered a period of extensive modernisation and expansion. During this period, new glass forming machines, lehrs (cooling chambers) and automatic inspection machines were installed as well as investment in new warehousing facilities. In 1971 no fewer than four of the nine furnaces within the company were rebuilt. At Barnsley eight section glass-forming machines were installed, which at the time was only the second machine of its type in the country.

Even more investment was needed and in1972 the company issued £1.5million 10per cent debenture stock in order to finance continuing development. As a result in the early 1970s unprecedented profits were recorded with the company employing over 3000 people in York and Barnsley.

death of his brother Harry in 1941, the average weight of a beverage container had decreased by 20 per cent by 1946, yet it was still as strong and held just as much as the earlier heavyweight version.

After the second world war it was decided that modernisation was needed, but that due to technical difficulties at Harborough Hills Road it was decided to make a fresh start on a new site.

The present site at Monk Bretton was two miles away and was chosen because of its direct rail access. The first sod was cut on 11th March 1946 by Milton Asquith, then Chairman and Managing Director, with production commencing on 12th June 1947. A steady programme of expansion took place over the next 20 years. By 1967 there were seven furnaces operating at Monk Bretton with only one left at the Old Mill Factory site.

The year 1967 also saw the last 'Lynch' bottle-making machine, first introduced in 1925, taken out of production.

It was also in 1967 that Redfearn Brothers Ltd merged with National Glass Ltd of York. The National Glass Works, located in Fishergate, York, had been established there in 1794, yet at the start of the 20th century the site had become disused and was acquired by a London glass merchant Charles Pratt. Mainly thanks to the efforts of William Pratt, Charles Pratt's son, by 1967 the York company had, like Redfearns, become a very prosperous business.

The new company was named Redfearn National Glass Limited and Anthony Barber

Top: *Milton Asquith cut the first sod of the Monk Bretton site, April 1st 1946.* *Below:* *Monk Bretton Glass Works starts to take shape.* *Inset:* *June 1947 and the Glass Works is ready for production to commence.*

at its Barnsley site, and began the hard climb upwards. Profitability was restored, and much needed investment could once again take place.

Encouraged by increased profitability the company decided in 1987 to diversify from glass and plastic containers and RNG plc acquired a flexible packaging company with premises in Bury, Lancashire, and Saffron Walden in Essex, becoming known as Redfearn Flexpack Ltd.

RNG now changed its name to Redfearn plc reflecting the increasing spread of its activities though more than half the company's business remained glass.

In March 1988 the final ties were broken with the company's past when John LC Pratt retired from the position of Chairman. During the same year the glass and flexibles operations were split with David Anderson taking on the role of Managing

By 1977 profits showed no sign of slackening and a new furnace capable of melting 350 metric tonnes of glass per day, the largest designed for the melting of green glass had been installed at the Barnsley Site. The following year a new batch mixing plan was built.

On 24th of August 1977, the first bottle bank was was opened in Barnsley and its prime motivator was Stanley Race, the then President of the Glass Manufacturer's Federation and Managing Director of Redfern National Glass. The event was broadcast by Yorkshire Television and Stanley Race was awarded the CBE in 1979 for his recycling efforts.

In 1980, the world saw a recession and combined with major competition from plastic containers in some of the traditional markets, the company saw a slump in sales.

By 1983 drastic action was needed and as a result the York site closed. Under a new Chief Executive, Arthur C Church, who was appointed in 1985, the company regrouped

Top: *From left to right: Coun. Jock Sturrock, Chairman of the Environment Committee of South Yorkshire County Council, Mr Stanley Race, President of the Glass Manufactures' Federation and Managing Director of Redfearn Nation Glass, and Coun. Kenneth Willers.*
Above right: *Rexam's new bottle bank.*
Right: *Duke of Kent and Chris Scholey, Managing Director of Rexam Glass Barnsley.*

Director for Glass and Mike Bradley Managing Director for Fleckpack.

The success of the company had again attracted interest and in December 1988 a takeover bid by the Swedish company PLM was successful and as a result the Redfearn became integrated into one of Europe's leading packaging company, being renamed PLM Redfearn.

Shortly after acquiring Redfearn's, PLM took the decision to focus on the core glass business and sold off the plastics division in January 1990 and not long afterwards agreed a management buy-out for the Flexpack business, leaving the Monk Bretton site as the sole UK division of PLM.

With no other products to distract it the Monk Bretton site could once again concentrate solely on producing glass containers on one of the largest glass manufacturing enterprises in Europe.

Redfearn became part of one of the largest European packaging companies, it gained access to technical, management, environmental and commercial skills of the highest order. Boundaries changed from supplying the UK to across Europe.

The PLM era saw heavy investment in all aspects of the company's operation, placing PLM Redfearn at the leading edge of glass packaging.

An important factor in the continued fortunes of the company since the 1980s decline was the development of decorative glass packaging ranges. In 1991 PLM Redfearn launched its Kaleidocoat decorative coating range and in 1998 saw the the launch of pressure sensitive labelling machines.

On 30th November 1998 Rexam plc put in a cash offer to PLM's shareholders and from 27th January PLM Redfearn became part of a global packaging company, Rexam plc.

In an effort to strengthen the Groups presence in all its markets throughout world it was decided that the entire group would be marketed using the same brand name. On the 3rd of April 2000 PLM Redfearn officially changed to Rexam Glass Barnsley.

In 2002 the company reached another landmark in its history with the 25th anniversary of the bottle bank scheme. Since that time the scheme has collected nationally, more than 6 million tonnes of recycled glass. Committed to green glass and a greener environment the company uses more than 50% of recycled material in its production process. Indeed in the green furnace the Monk Bretton site uses of 85% recycled material, simultaneously succeeding to use less energy, creating fewer emissions and reducing the need for quarrying for raw materials.

Today as Rexam Glass, the company is proud of its long tenure in Barnsley and its place in local history stretch back more than a century. The future will no doubt be as absorbing as the past. Rexam cannot predict its future but if you consider the first recorded output was 1152 bottles per day for one bottle making team against 500,000 from one of today's modern bottle making machines the company can only look forward to advancements in years to come.

Top left: *The production of bottles at Rexam Glass, circa 1999.* ***Below:*** *A birds eye view of Rexam Glass, Monk Bretton.*

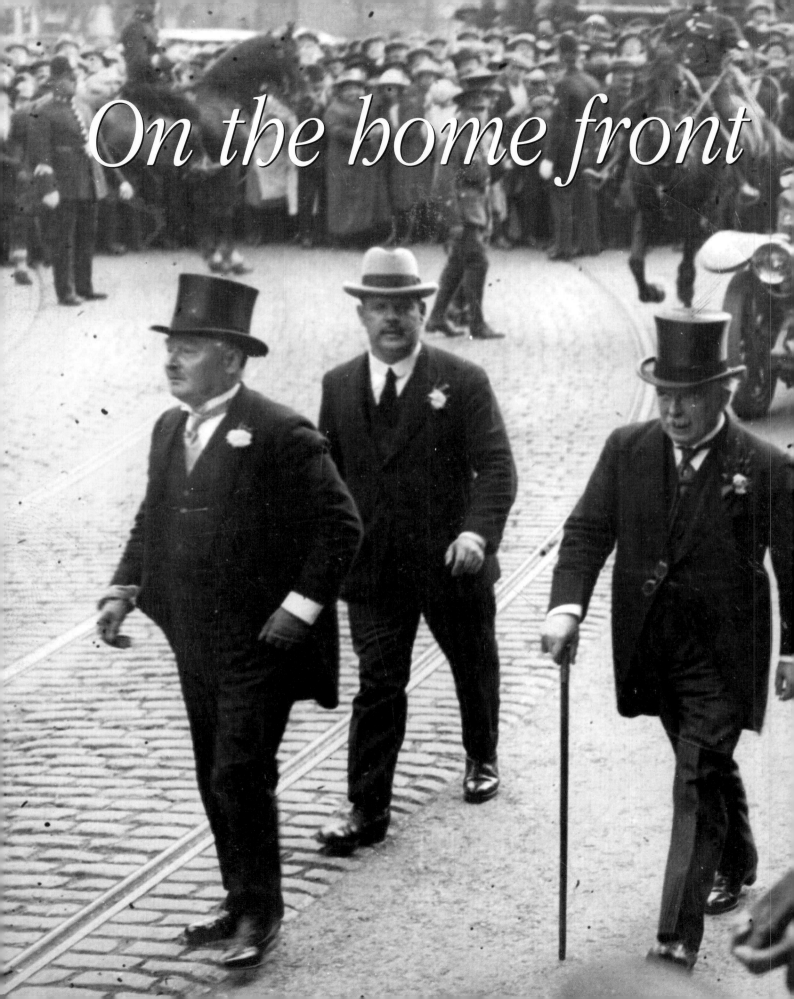

On the home front

Eldon Street was used to witnessing large crowds as processions regularly passed along this road and it was often the centre for large rallies. An enormous throng turned out to listen to the Salvationist General Booth when he visited in 1905 and the numbers were repeated on this occasion on 27 August 1921. Prime Minister David Lloyd George, cutting a dash with his top hat and walking cane, thanked the men from the York and Lancaster Regiment for their noble service during the Great War. These brave chaps had seen action in the bloodiest parts of the European theatre and had also experienced the nightmare of Gallipoli during the costly Dardanelles campaign. Lloyd George rose to the highest political office in Britain in 1916, following the resignation of Herbert Asquith. He had already carved out a name for himself as the longest serving Chancellor of the Exchequer the country had ever had, a record only broken in 2004 by Gordon Brown. Some of those forming the guard of honour harboured reservations about their Prime Minister, though. After all, it was under his leadership that the action at Passchendaele in 1917 was sanctioned and an estimated 325,000 soldiers lost their lives for little apparent territorial gain. Although many in the crowd raised their hats and cheered Lloyd George there were others who muttered darkly about the slow arrival of the land fit for heroes that they had been promised.

Above: The popular BBC TV sitcom 'Dad's Army' made audiences laugh in the 1970s and 1980s. Repeats in later years were no less successful. The country's living rooms rocked to viewers' merriment at the antics of a Home Guard unit run by a pompous bank manager. Its members included old soldiers, an undertaker, a butcher and a trainee bank clerk. That much was accurate. They were just the sort of people that volunteered to join a force entrusted with guarding key installations and sworn to protect those left at home by service personnel fighting overseas. The rest of the television series did not do them justice. The Home Guard was not the bumbling outfit as portrayed by the fictitious Warmington on Sea platoon. Admittedly, when initially formed as the Local Defence Volunteers, some early efforts were ridiculous. One platoon patrolled with imitation rifles once used in a Drury Lane production. Elsewhere catapults were recommended as launching pads for petrol bombs, and broomsticks were converted into pikes when knives were attached. The force was renamed the Home Guard in July 1940 and 250,000 men were enrolled. Although still handicapped by a shortage of weapons and resources, they trained with vigour and initiative. Here, Barnsley men held their rifles and bayonets with pride as the inspection party passed among their ranks. Their resolve was just as firm as any enlisted man and that determination to keep the enemy at bay was etched on every face.

Below: It was the inspirational performance of the Royal Air Force during the late summer of 1940 that caused Hitler to postpone his plans for Operation Sea Lion, the invasion of Britain. To gain the upper hand, the Luftwaffe had to dominate the skies and provide protection for the incoming flotilla. The success of our brave pilots meant that our shores would never be breached during the six year conflict that was the second world war. Prime Minister Churchill was moved to say, 'Never in the field of human conflict was so much owed by so many to so few.' An inspection parade of local Air Training Corps (ATC) cadets took place in the glow of the uplifting example of those who had taken part in the aerial Battle of Britain. The ATC was formed by royal warrant in 1941 and sprang from the Air Defence Cadet Corps founded in 1938 by the Air League. Some of these boys had to grow into men almost overnight as they proudly went to serve king and country. We owe an immense debt to such as these, many of who never made it into true adulthood. The ATC still flourishes today, giving youngsters a sense of purpose and an opportunity to consider life in the RAF as a possible career move. With almost 35,000 members, aged from 13 to 22, in its 1,000 squadrons it is one of the country's premier youth organisations.

Shopping spree

It is difficult to identify this part of town with just a quick glance at this photograph that dates from the 1920s. Once called Kirkgate, this is Church Street as it looked 80 years ago. The rather dapper couple in the foreground appear to be quite comfortably off, if the cut of their clothes is any evidence as they pass A Wright's chemist shop that opened in 1923. His sharp, three piece suit is quite elegantly cut and his lady looks to be smartly and expensively dressed. The hat is a delightful period piece with its cloche shape and brim shading her eyes. Her skirt length is significant. A few years before the war she would have worn it down to ground level, but now it just covers her knees. This displays her flouting of convention and the push by women for equality born of the suffragette years. The fur stole is possibly expensive sable or perhaps a fox pelt. Such adornments typify the well to do of the flapper age. Animals did not have rights in that era. From about 1929 onwards the property on the right, including Whaley Brothers' furnishers, established in 1894, was demolished to make way for the Town Hall. The Royal Hotel on the left, now called The Assembly, still stands. Formerly the White Bear Inn, it changed its name in 1835 following a visit from the Duchess of Kent and Princess Victoria.

Above: The woman in the 1958 view of a rather shambolic Shambles Street appears to have been startled by the sound of the camera's shutter, turning to stare rather suspiciously at whoever it is that is interested in capturing her image. She had just come past Blenkinsop's, a name that featured on this shop front for 75 years. William G Blenkinsop sold confectionery here (1884-1914) until G Blenkinsop turned it into a pork butcher's. He sold up in 1959 to Green's Radio and that business was still in place when the demolition men moved in during 1963. Not before time, most people thought, as this row of shops was long past its sell by date. Don Valley, the self styled 'modern cleaners and dyers', opened for business in 1950 and continued to trade here until the bitter end. The shop had formerly been Braithwaite's grocery store, first trading from here in 1902. The woman in view was heading towards the paper merchant and Bull's Head Yard further up Shambles Street from the cleaner's. Three Threes, being advertised on the hoarding, was a brand that some might remember. Manufactured by State Express, at one time the packets contained cigarette cards that have become collectors' items. Particularly popular now at antique fairs is the 1935 sporting hero series featuring such great names as Don Bradman, Fred Perry, Len Harvey and Gordon Richards.

Below: Postwar Britain was a largely gloomy place. We had won the war but now had to pay the cost. Rationing continued, divorce rates went through the roof, spare cash was hard to come by and we all had to tighten our belts. Even by the early 1950s of this scene on Eldon Street, the austerity of those times still affected our daily lives. Still, you could dream. None more so than young lovers who made their way to Harral's. Any young man who had no thought of marriage used to stay well clear of this part of town when with his girlfriend. If she suggested coming this way he had a diversion planned out. But for those in love, it was a wonderful place to be. Generations of sweethearts bought their engagement and wedding rings here. Some men who should have known better also bought their secretaries little keepsakes, but we had better gloss over those activities. The delightful façade of this shop was so well known that people used to make the spot underneath the clock a popular place to meet up with friends. Benjamin Harral previously owned a shop further along Eldon Street, nearer to the Market Hall, identified by a sign that had a ring painted on it. When he built these premises he simply called them The Ring Shop. It ceased trading in 1988, becoming an estate agent's. S Tetley and Son traded as a tobacconist in the neighbouring building from 1926-57 before becoming Saxone's shoe shop.

Below: The winter of 1955-56 was full of the usual doom and gloom that the newspapers loved to report. Princess Margaret had ditched her fiancé, Group Captain Peter Townsend, because of establishment disapproval of her romance with a divorced man. Shades of the 1936 abdication crisis, it would seem. South African delegates walked out of a United Nations debate on apartheid, Rosa Parks was fined in Alabama for refusing to move from a whites only part of a bus, British soldiers were killed by EOKA terrorists in Cyprus and the bank rate soared to its highest since 1931. Not that any of this had much effect on the determined march of the housewives striding out purposefully along Cheapside. They were passing a branch of the Co-op that had established its impressive central premises at Island Corner, at the top of New Street. These women adopted headscarves as a halfway house between the expense of having a hat and the unlady-like practice of going about bareheaded. The headscarf was pooh-poohed by the more hoity-toity folk who preferred to display their airs and graces and put a designer number on top of their perms that cost five times more than a Toni applied at home. They had a shock when the Queen was photographed at Sandringham wearing, would you believe, a headscarf. My oh my, whatever was the world coming to? Thin ends and wedges were discussed.

Right: The market was in full swing, with all its associated traders' cries and produce smells drifting on the air. Market Hill, with Church Street beyond, was full of hustle and bustle on this typical day from c1953, the year of the Coronation, the ascent of Everest and the Stanley Matthews' FA Cup Final. The Town Hall behind the market stalls has dominated this part of town since the early 1930s. If visitors to Barnsley remember just one thing about the town, it is this stunning architectural masterpiece. Others might comment on the gradient as they puff up the hill from Eldon Street, as the climb up to where the road levels out near Regent Street can tax the lungs of those who are a little out of condition. The Luton-bodied delivery van, on the left, and the various other saloons dotted around the picture look like the little Dinky cars we played with as children in later years. If only we had put them on a shelf and retained their boxes those toys would be worth a small fortune to collectors today. Notice the shades of the coachwork on the motorcars. Nearly all conform to Henry Ford's comment that you could have any colour you wanted as long as it was black. Fancy colours and even fancier names for them were for the next generation of motoring.

Above: The Sunday School mounted the late 1960s display in Pitt Street Methodist Church interesting the elderly couple. This was quite a religious area of town with St George's Church, the Salem Chapel, Blucher Street Chapel, the Temperance Hall and the Wesleyan Chapel all situated within a stone's throw of one another. It was a Sunday School that obviously believed in the ethic of healthy bodies as well as healthy minds. All manner of outdoor and indoor sporting equipment was on display, from tennis and badminton racquets to skis and dinghies. Outward bound pursuits and activity based ventures such as the Duke of Edinburgh Scheme for young people were very popular before they discovered the art of flopping in front of a video player or jabbing away at buttons on a Playstation. The interest in widening their experience was not confined to this country. There was a chance to take part in a German exchange holiday. This type of opportunity to learn about the culture of our European cousins at first hand was a growing trend, though France was more often the choice. Youngsters stayed with a foreign family for a week or so and a child from that house paid a return visit some weeks later in a sort of Barnsley meets Bonn exercise. Not everyone was completely taken with the idea of the German exchange as the couple looking at the display remembered that our countries were deadly enemies just 20 years earlier.

Below: Various groups linked with Pitt Street Methodists mounted displays in the church on an occasion in the late 1960s that gave a flavour of what their organisations were about. This section was given over to the Girl Guides. Youngsters in this movement, even in the early days, dedicated themselves to a mixture of recreational and instructional activities. Robert Baden-Powell's sister, Agnes, and his wife, Olave, were the prime movers in generating the interest that led to the international appeal of guiding. Recognised by the trefoil design for membership badges patented in 1914, women, long past their active guiding years who may now be members of the Trefoil Guild, have been known to display their insignia on their lapels well into their advancing years. They fondly remember the joy of togetherness with their youthful peers and, especially, the camps they attended. That was obviously the case for the Pitt Street girls as well, because the tent takes pride of place in this exhibition. Do they still reserve a special moment for Thinking Day every 22nd of February, a date established in 1926? Girl Guides were given the royal seal of approval in 1937 when Queen Elizabeth, later best known as the late Queen Mother, became the association's official patron and Princess Margaret enrolled as a Brownie. The Queen's Guide Award was introduced in 1946 and Queen Elizabeth II became joint patron with her mother in 1952.

Right: Building of the market complex was taking place during July 1972 on Cheapside. The focus of the town's market on Market Hill, where the street just down from the Town Hall was once alive with throngs of shoppers, changed with this development programme. The old Court House Station car park was used as a temporary trading area as the building work went on. Barnsley was granted a charter to hold an annual fair and weekly market in 1249 by Henry III. The monks of Pontefract administered these until Henry VIII dissolved the monasteries in the 16th century. May Day Green was regularly buzzing with commercial activity. The early markets gave farmers the opportunity to centralise their point of sale, but they became bigger than just fruit and vegetable outlets. Livestock was traded and, by the 18th century, linen and other household goods were common-place on the stalls. These markets also attracted entertainers, such as jugglers, fire eaters and acrobats who then passed a hat round for donations. Less savoury characters came along, too, as market day was a fine opportunity for pickpockets to make a killing or for thieves to lie in wait and rob a trader or farmer on his way home. At one time Barnsley market was the largest open air one in northern England. In the late 1940s it covered an area of nearly four acres and was split between six sites: May Day Green, Lower May Day Green, Market Hill, New Market, Queen's and Kendray.

Below: Looking down from the Town Hall on a chilly 20 January 1971, we are gazing across Shambles Street and down Market Hill. In the distance a crane hovers above Eldon Street, about to do its worst as it did away with the old to bring in the new in the belief that all change was for the good. What a pity that we lost some of our favourite buildings and the memories they held during this time of modernisation. Although some of the names on the businesses have altered, at least the scene we are witnessing in this picture has hardly changed, though the market stalls have gone. The Halifax Building Society on the corner of Shambles Street was built where the Corn Exchange stood until ravaged by fire in 1927. It is now the rather foolishly named Blah Bar. Opposite, at 1-5 Church Street, was the elegant façade of Butterfields and Massies. 'Butterfield's Drapery Market' is still the inscription over the door, despite its closure in 1975, and is a permanent reminder of the business' origins. Inside the department store older shoppers might recall the network of overhead wires that helped transport money and receipts between the tills and the cashier's office. The store was run by successive generations of the families, starting in the 1830s. This site, once used by Ludlam's mercers in Stuart times and Henry and Joseph's drapers in the Georgian era, is now called The Australian Bar. Presumably, it sells koalaburgers. Further down the hill, Henry Elstone's, established in 1797, sold tobacco, cigars, pipes, newspapers and fancy chocolates.

Above: Market day around May Day Green in the late 1960s was a popular time to get your bargain shopping done. The stalls were laden with goods and fresh produce as the traders called out to potential customers with witty or encouraging cries in an effort to attract their attention. They also wanted to loosen a few purse strings, but first they had to bring them within reach. Some of the housewives, and there were still very many who did not object to that description, had evidently completed their day's shopping. Laden down with bags that threatened to lengthen their arms permanently by a couple of inches, they moved off to catch the bus home. How times have changed. Once women consigned their bras to the ceremonial pyre, being called 'a housewife' was regarded as a demeaning term. A decade earlier it was a fond form of address. The invalid carriage in the foreground was a period piece. They gave disabled people an element of freedom, releasing them from being tied to the house and completely reliant upon others. The down side was that the carriages were far from sturdy and provided little protection to their occupants in an accident. They could also become unstable in high winds and even a sudden gust made them wobble about alarmingly.

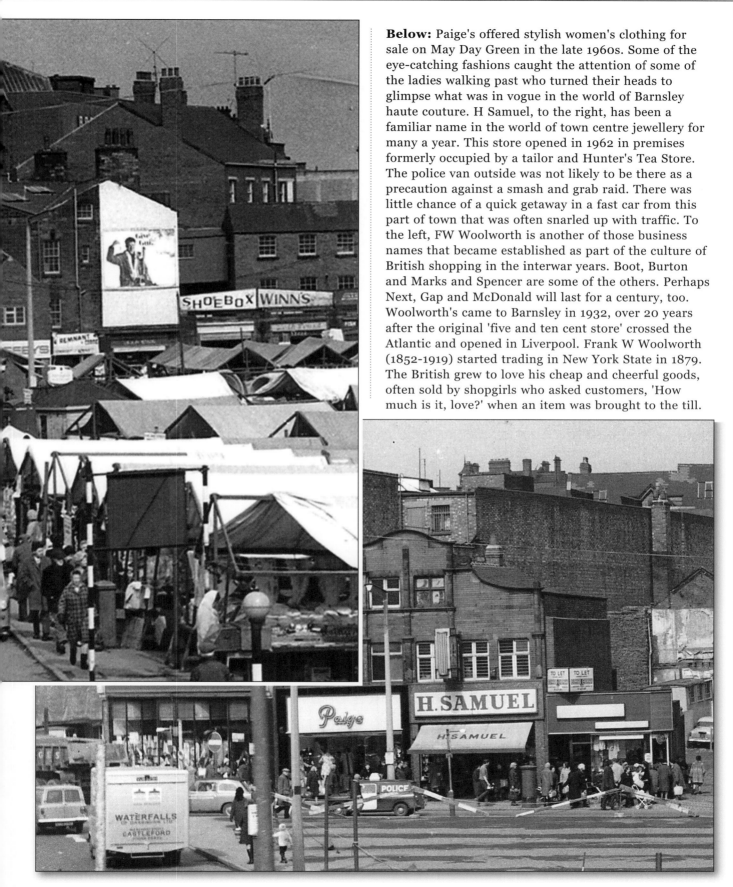

Below: Paige's offered stylish women's clothing for sale on May Day Green in the late 1960s. Some of the eye-catching fashions caught the attention of some of the ladies walking past who turned their heads to glimpse what was in vogue in the world of Barnsley haute couture. H Samuel, to the right, has been a familiar name in the world of town centre jewellery for many a year. This store opened in 1962 in premises formerly occupied by a tailor and Hunter's Tea Store. The police van outside was not likely to be there as a precaution against a smash and grab raid. There was little chance of a quick getaway in a fast car from this part of town that was often snarled up with traffic. To the left, FW Woolworth is another of those business names that became established as part of the culture of British shopping in the interwar years. Boot, Burton and Marks and Spencer are some of the others. Perhaps Next, Gap and McDonald will last for a century, too. Woolworth's came to Barnsley in 1932, over 20 years after the original 'five and ten cent store' crossed the Atlantic and opened in Liverpool. Frank W Woolworth (1852-1919) started trading in New York State in 1879. The British grew to love his cheap and cheerful goods, often sold by shopgirls who asked customers, 'How much is it, love?' when an item was brought to the till.

Bird's eye view

This 1929 aerial photograph was taken showing the Perseverance estate, in between Summer Lane Station to the left and Dodworth Road to the right. Barnsley was not exclusively a mining town, though much of its economy was linked with coal. In this busy part of town, to the west of the centre, were such diverse businesses as an abattoir, Gillott and Son's Lancaster Works, Qualters and Smith Brothers' engineers, McLintock's quilt manufacturing company and many warehouses. This was a very active part of Barnsley, with a genuine working class feel. Industry, transport and housing all blended together in an atmosphere of mutual support and co-existence. Through history, Barnsley has had a variety of commercial interests. It built a reputation as a centre for linen weaving in the 18th century, with a concentration of mills around Town End by the middle of the following century. Over 400 steam looms were in operation in Taylor's Mill on Peel Street in the 1880s. There was also a thriving glass industry. The Redfearns established their works at Old Mill in 1862, producing innovative glass-stoppered bottles. In this century, the construction company MP Burke is the largest production employer, but the greatest number of jobs overall are with the local authority and the NHS. In 1929, Britain was still struggling to regain its prewar position as a major economic power. It was plunged further into depression by the year end when the American stock market crashed. Few on the Perseverance estate held shares, but their employers relied on investment markets to help with stability and expansion.

This aerial view was taken in 1933. It shows the junction of Park Grove and Hawthorne Street in the foreground. The school on Agnes Road is to the left and Park Road in the centre as we look southeast. Today, we would say that it was a view towards the M1. What a sea of terraced property we had. Row after row of housing, much of which would have been occupied by people with a working link to mining. They were tightly knit communities where families and neighbours looked out for each other. Children referred to the adults next door as 'aunty' and 'uncle', keeping that small note of reserve and respect for their elders that is now lost. As well as their adoptive relatives on the block, youngsters usually did not have too far to go when visiting blood relations. Grannies, cousins, nephews and nieces often lived close by because most people stayed close to their roots. Some Barnsley folk moved away from the town to seek fame and fortune, but they were in the minority. However, the town is proud of those who furthered Barnsley's reputation by their achievements elsewhere. Michael Parkinson worked for several local newspapers before coming to national notice as a journalist and columnist with the Manchester Guardian, Observer and Sunday Times. His television work has been a masterclass for aspiring talk show hosts for 35 years. Parky's Yorkshire accent is still with him and that is something satisfying for those of us who despise people who try to disguise their origins.

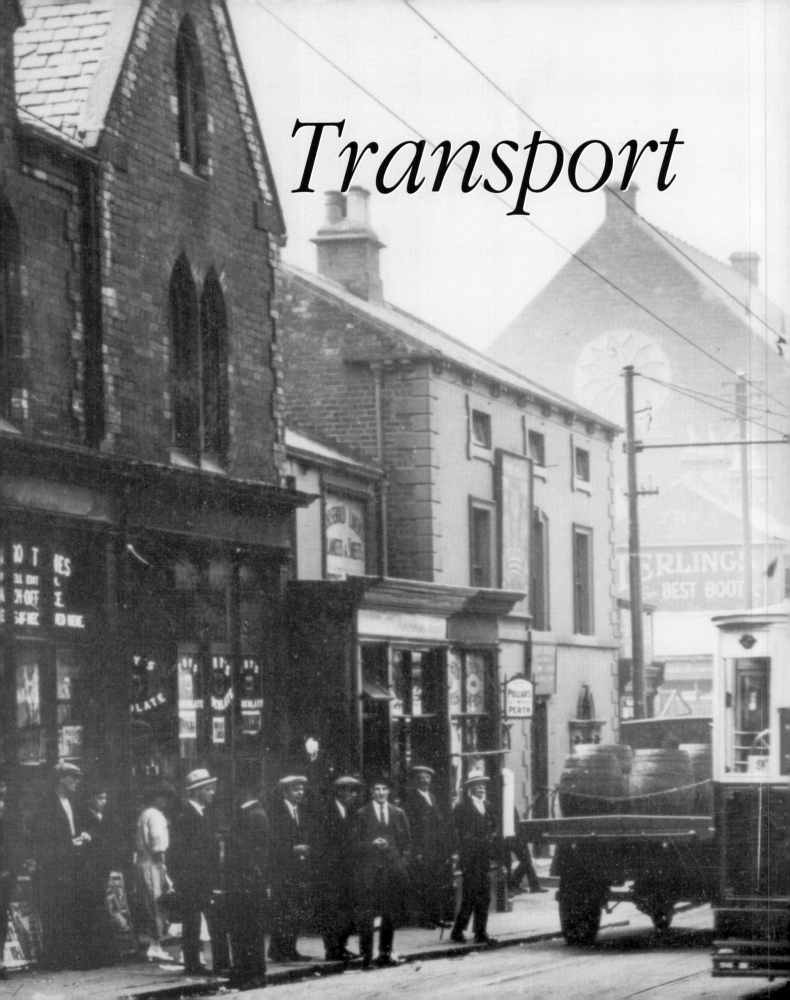

Transport

The electric tram on Wombwell High Street was not quite up to the class of the one that inspired Judy Garland to break into song in the 1944 film 'Meet me in St Louis', but it seemed to be attracting the attention of the men on the pavement. Readers might have thought that their attention would have been directed towards the brewery dray, but this was obviously a sober set of locals. Before motorbuses took over, trams were a major boon to public transport and helped provide a steady stream of shoppers into Wombwell for which retailers were truly happy. The little motorcycle and sidecar was a common sight on our roads in the days when grandpa was a lad. How could any girl resist a seat in such luxury transport? Quite easily, was often the answer on cold, wet and windy days. This form of motoring was widely adopted by the RAC and AA organisations and in use long after the second world war. Mechanics flitted about the countryside coming to the rescue of stranded members as radiators boiled over and fuel pumps failed. At one time these riders saluted members who displayed their organisation's badge on the car bonnet, though the practice was eventually abandoned so that both hands could be kept on the handlebars. Old fashioned courtesy gave way to the demands of the health and safety thought police.

Above: The laundry van, about to overtake the horse and cart, was just passing the Town Hall on 8 February 1950. We are reliably informed that it was just half an hour before noon when the photograph was taken. Perhaps that was the exact moment recorded by the ambulance driver attending the accident that surely would have occurred with a photographer standing in the middle of Church Street! The handsome building on the right, on the corner of Regent Street, belongs to Barnsley Permanent Building Society. Frederick Goodyear, the society's president, laid the foundation stone for this fine edifice on 7 November 1935. It opened for business the following year. Barclays Bank is further along, just past Dow Passage. It dates from 1916, being built on the site of former premises that had banking connections going back to 1796. The Mining and Technical College on the left opened in 1932. It gave training in construction, electrical engineering, commercial subjects, the sciences and technical drawing, but it is the mining aspect that is the most important part of the name as it reminds us of the debt we owe to the coal industry. For so many years individual mining companies, followed by the National Coal Board, later British Coal, dominated the provision of jobs for Barnsley workers. A quarter of the population was employed in the industry, even as late as 1981. That employment has gone, but the three main buildings in the picture have changed little in appearance or function since they were built.

Below: Goodness only knows where Mr Strong, the pedlar, had got to but, presumably, he was somewhere on board the cart that was a familiar sight on Peel Street in the mid 1950s. Since he was renowned for enjoying a drink or two he could have been snoozing quietly, curled up somewhere among the mops, bottles, pots, pans and other paraphernalia that he hawked on his round. His horse was well used to finding its way home without any direction from him as it had delivered its snoring master safely on more than one occasion in the past. Although we were in the second half of the 20th century the horse and cart was still a familiar, if occasional, sight on our streets. As well as Mr Strong selling his wares, there were gypsies driving around with clothes pegs and lucky heather for sale, as well as offering to carry out odd jobs around the house and garden. Totters, with their penetrating 'rag-bone' cry, roamed the streets collecting odds and ends from housewives in return for a donkeystone with which they could brighten the appearance of their front doorstep. Gardeners were particularly keen to know when the horses were approaching so that they could get a bucket out of the shed. The keener ones followed behind the cart for as long as it took for Dobbin to leave a calling card that would benefit the roses and rhubarb.

Above: The single decker bus turning into Regent Street, passing the ornamental pillars of the Barnsley Permanent Building Society, was heading towards Court House Station at lunchtime on 11 February 1950. Housewives on board muttered about the privations caused by yet another cut in the weekly meat ration. With rump steak selling at an inflated 2s 8d (13p) per pound, the ration represented a mere four ounces of meat per week, or five ounces if buying imported lamb chops. Butchers estimated that it would take three ration books to buy a pound of meat and at least a dozen for a leg of lamb. The allowance was now at its lowest ever and to think we had actually won the war. Shortages meant that the black marketers made easy profits. The double decker travelling up Church Street advertised Hovis, reminding those of us brought up as baby boomers of the halfpenny mini Hovis loaves fresh from the oven. Scrumptious! The other advert for Vernon's Pools gave punters a chance to indulge in flights of get rich quick fantasy. Every Saturday they sat beside their wirelesses listening to Sports Report at five o'clock. They checked their coupons for the magical eight draws as the results were read out. Five minutes later it was a case of never mind, there is always next week.

Below: Littlewood's Pools is part of the empire belonging to the Moores family from Merseyside. It was the major company of those that invited us to forecast football results each week in the hope that the treble chance, as it was called, would bring us fortune and a little fame. In the 1960s one celebrated winner, Viv Nicholson, announced that she was going to 'Spend, spend, spend'. She did just that and blew the lot in a year. Vernon's and Zetter's also ran similar football pools, but were second division in comparison to Littlewood's. Since the birth of the National Lottery, this soccer based style of modest gambling has struggled to compete. The Yorkshire Traction double decker in the photograph is seen on the morning of 21 January 1950, heading into Regent Street towards the Congregational Church, built in 1856. It is about to pass the old Post Office. Solicitors and firms offering financial services occupy many of the buildings along this part of Regent Street. Parts of it now look rather drab and gloomy. The single decker turning into Church Street bore the registration letters HE. These showed that it had first been registered in Barnsley. The motor cyclist on the right was well wrapped up against the weather, but his headgear was quite lightweight. Compulsory crash helmets were some way to the future.

Working life

Below: The rebuilding of Beevor Hill Bridge on Pontefract Road was undertaken in 1926. These workmen had no need of hard hats. The ubiquitous working man's flat cap was good enough for them. Their usual heavy duty boots were enough protective footwear and, if they had the good luck and the strength to survive the trenches in France and Belgium a decade earlier, the dangers of bridge building paled in comparison. To the layman, this jumble of concrete, reinforcing wire, steel girders and timber spars seems a mystery. Quite how it all fits together seems to be puzzling one of the workmen staring down in front of him but, as if by magic, it all took shape. We should not be surprised as Britain has a tremendous tradition in engineering. Names like Telford, Brunel and Stephenson spring readily to mind, but Barnsley has a worthy servant to the industrial revolution of its own in Joseph Locke (1805-60). Born in Attercliffe, he moved to Barnsley at the age of five. He was apprenticed to George Stephenson in 1823 and worked on the Stockton-Darlington and Liverpool-Manchester railways. His skill saw him become the chief engineer for the Grand Junction Railway and was heavily involved in the town planning of Crewe. He also designed the railway line from Manchester to Sheffield that included the three mile Woodhead Tunnel. He became president of the Institute of Civil Engineers in 1857. His wife dedicated Locke Park to his memory in 1862.

The majority of British workmen in 1934 dressed in almost uniform clothing. This gang of labourers, despite being involved in heavy manual work, favoured white, collarless shirts worn under waistcoats. A few might have had a muffler draped around their necks and nearly all sported that icon of the working class male, the flat cap. The foreman usually made sure that he could be recognised as being a cut above the rest. The man on the left with the jacket and homburg was, in all probability, the one overseeing the relaying of girders and the mixing of concrete. The gang was working on the rebuilding of Pogmoor Bridge on Pogmoor Road, just north of Dodworth Road. The workforce must have been glad of the employment as jobs outside the mines were hard to come by. The dole queues stood at one million at the start of the decade, but by the early 30s had tripled as Britain faced the darkest years of the Depression. All over the country unrest fomented and riots and protest marches were regular occurrences. Oswald Mosley's British Union of Fascists took the opportunity to whip up racial hatred, particularly against the Jews, as Britons tried to find somebody to blame for their parlous state. The men on Pogmoor Bridge had little time for such extremists and bent their backs, anxious to do a good job and thankful that they could tip up their wage packets onto the kitchen table at the end of the week.

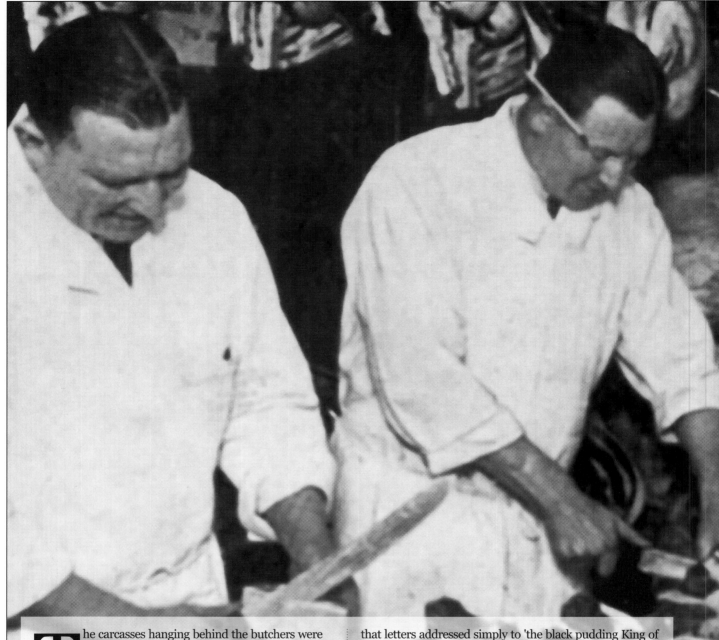

The carcasses hanging behind the butchers were carefully cut into steaks, joints and sides with consummate skill. That was hardly surprising as the Hirst brothers were masters of their trade in the interwar years. The more famous of the two, Albert (on the right), was especially known for his black puddings, calling them 'the north's caviar'. His concoctions won cups and medals in a variety of championships, though the world championship held in Montagne-au-Perche always eluded him. However, the French have never been too keen in accepting English culinary skills or our meat and there was some suspicion about continental bias in the judging. At home, Albert became so famous that letters addressed simply to 'the black pudding King of England' always arrived. Pictured on 13 December 1933, the Hirsts were working in the Royal Hotel kitchens, preparing Barnsley chops that were to be served the following day to the Prince of Wales at the ceremonial opening of the Town Hall. It is said that the future Edward VIII blanched at the thought of having to consume a 3lb cut of mutton. The Barnsley chop is thought to have originated in the King's Head Hotel, where the Nat West bank now stands. Farmers going to market made a tradition of lunching on large chops, though they usually limited themselves to those about half the weight of the one that caused such royal consternation.

Above: The car driving along Old Mill Lane in 1936 was a real period piece with its rear mounted spare wheel and running boards. You could almost picture Al Capone's men standing on these boards as they machine-gunned their way through the streets of Chicago during prohibition in America a few years earlier. Thankfully, Barnsley did not need 'the untouchables' to police its streets. A couple of the boys in blue with truncheons sufficed quite nicely. The workmen were busy widening the railway bridge and realigning the road as part of an improvement scheme. An inspector of works, marked out by his suit and bowler hat, was checking that everything conformed to plan. It was hard, sweaty work, but these labourers were well used to that. They were not afraid to get their hands dirty, even if the inspector made sure that his clothes and fingernails remained free from grime. He was a boss after all and, as far as the working class was concerned, came from an environment and a world that was totally alien to their own. Labourers knew their place in society and were destined to spend a life in toil that gave them just enough in their wage packets to feed the family and pay the rent. However, there was no permanency of employment and there were periods out of work when they had to struggle along on the meagre benefits the state provided. Dole money was a pittance in 1936.

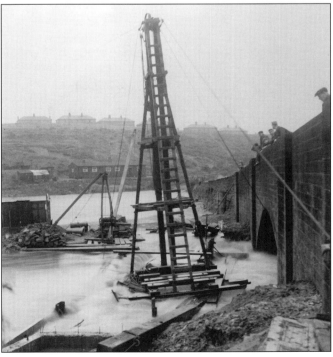

Left: The men peering over the bridge on the A628 Pontefract Road in 1930, near Hoyle Mill, were taking in the amount of damage caused by floodwater as the River Dearne was in spate, yet again. Those who had jobs knew that they would be joining the ranks of the unemployed for a while and there were enough of those already. Unemployment in Britain doubled in a year to a staggering 2 million. Little did this small knot of men know, but there was worse to come as the decade unfolded. By the end of 1932, the jobless numbered nearly 3 million, with all the attendant misery that brought. It was just as well that these men could not see the future in the murky waters of the Dearne. The river itself is a fairly modest affair, but it is Barnsley's river and a tricky quiz question for pub teams from outside Yorkshire. During the days when the coalfields and steel plants dominated the landscape, the Dearne was heavily polluted. As most of this heavy industry has now disappeared, the countryside in the valley has become more attractive and the river much cleaner. Fish can swim in its waters without gasping for air and positive steps have been taken in recent years to increase these stocks.

Top left: Navigation was suspended on the River Dearne until work on the new Cliffe Bridge was completed in 1930. The river became part of the Dearne and Dove Canal in the late 18th century, constructed under the leadership of its chief engineer, Robert Mylne. He was only the second choice as the feted William Jessop declined the job because of pressures of work on other projects. The full length of the waterway took 11 years to complete and its locks, loops and rises were a credit to the skill of our forefathers. The cost of the project came to £100,000, way over budget, and a figure that would equate to many millions today. The main purpose of the canal was to ferry coal, particularly to Lincolnshire, but other commodities were carried as well. Limestone, pig iron, timber and corn all found their places on board the barges. By 1810, the Dearne and Dove carried an annual cargo of over 73,000 tons, rising to 181,000 tons by 1830 with 70 barges travelling along the canal each week. The arrival of the railway in 1840 put paid to the heydays of this form of transport. Trade decreased as rail won the competition for business and, with repair and maintenance costs escalating, the Dearne and Dove went into decline. Sheffield and South Yorkshire Navigation was formed as a new company to run the canal in 1894, but abandonment of sections began in 1906. Subsidence caused by mining created several breaches and further stretches were closed in the 1920s. Most of the main line closed in 1934 and the last section near Barnsley came to an end in 1942. Odd portions remain, but official abandonment took place in 1961.

Above: Most people refer to such a fuel container as a gasometer but, to be pedantic, it is actually a gasholder. In 1936 it provided a backdrop to the work taking place on the bridge widening on Old Mill Lane. The gang looks to be somewhat precariously placed, but their footing was more secure than that of the monarch in Buckingham Palace. This was the year that saw us serving three kings. George V died in January and was replaced by his eldest son who became Edward VIII. Although common knowledge in the gossip columns abroad, his relationship with the twice divorced American socialite Wallis Simpson was kept from the majority of the British public. Newspapers kept their counsel, unlike modern tabloids that would have banner headlines reinforced by salacious photographs in a similar situation nowadays. Things came to a head when King Edward decided that he wanted to marry his lover. The establishment was shocked and the Church of England horrified. Eventually, the lid could not be kept on the scandal any longer. The nation's opinion was sharply divided between those who felt that Edward should follow his heart and those who thought that he should toe the traditional, moral line and rid himself of a gold digger who once said 'a woman can never be too rich or too thin'. In December, the King abdicated and his brother became George VI. All of these shenanigans mattered little to the workers on Old Mill Lane Bridge. Whatever the regal outcome, there was one life for the la-di-dah and another for men in braces and cloth caps.

Above: This section of Sheffield Road, below Park Road, underwent resurfacing in June 1954. The advert on the billboard, telling us that 'a little Bovril goes a long way', might make some of us think of Saturday afternoons spent on the freezing terraces at Oakwell, clutching a steaming cup of the meaty extract in icy fingers as we supported our home town team. The little lad on the pavement watching the men at work would have been subjected to a variety of brews recommended for his good health. Horlicks, Ovaltine, Bovril and Oxo all had their supporters for one reason or another. As a toddler he was also entitled to NHS orange juice, that thick, sweet syrup that was one of the free benefits of the welfare state introduced under the Labour government after the war. This youngster, presumably then out with his grandparents, is one of the baby boomer generation and will now be in his late 50s. Rationing had just finished when he watched the steamroller flatten the tarmac and he was to reap the benefits of the better years that came as the nation moved from the harsh times of the immediate postwar years into the security of the Macmillan 'never had it so good' era of the late 1950s and early 1960s. What happened to this lad? Did he find fame and fortune or was he one of the mining fraternity of the 1980s crushed by Thatcher just as surely as the gravel under the roller's wheel on Sheffield Road?

Below: As a nation we just love to stand and watch other people at work. Quite what is so entertaining about observing a group of workers resurfacing a road is hard to fathom, but these men shovelling away for all they were worth had quite an audience. The A61 Sheffield Road in June 1954 was a busy main road, so the traffic jams caused by the roadworks must have been frustrating for motorists. They might as well have got used to sitting in their cars on a stop-start journey because motoring would be like that for the next 50 years and more. This was the start of the age of the family saloon. Once the preserve of the middle classes, private car ownership took off in the late 1950s. Names like Popular, Prefect, Minx, Minor, Elf and Imp were some of those used for the models that appeared outside front gates on ordinary streets where once there might have been an occasional motorbike and sidecar. That summer of half a century ago heralded a new order in many aspects of life. Athletes broke the four minute barrier for the mile, youth had its day in the Derby when a young jockey called Lester Piggott was victorious and the Eurovision television service was launched. Ration books were ceremonially torn up on 3 July and the country looked forward to greater prosperity in a new Elizabethan Age.

Right: The Town Hall was framed by what remained of the shell of the tithe Barn on Westgate in January 1968. The barn, situated in between Stanhope Yard and the Stores Yard, had a butcher's shop incorporated into its front. At the time, this part of town was given over to a collection of warehouses, barns, shops, storage yards and ageing houses, all of which had seen better days. Tithe is the old English for a tenth and has its origins in the church, but the practice of contributing that fraction of a person's income for religious purposes goes back to the Old Testament. It was adopted by Christianity as a means of providing an income for the clergy and maintenance for the churches. It was made obligatory under ecclesiastical law in Britain in the 10th century, becoming part of our temporal laws fairly soon afterwards when the Crown realised the simplicity and value of such a tax to the establishment. Farming communities often contributed produce or stock instead of money. Some landowners adopted the church's practice and used tithes as a means of collecting rent. Tithes continued to be collected by the Church of England until 1836 when they were commuted to rent charges dependent upon the price of grain. It was not until as recently as 1936 that these were officially abolished.

Bottom left: On 22 October 1970 work was well under way on the construction of the Grange Bridge floodwater sewer on Grange Lane, over the River Dearne. 'About time, too,' thought the residents in the bungalows in the background. Earlier that year they had been washed out in the springtime floods that were a common feature of life for those living along the valley plain. While the construction work took place the locals had to put up with lorries laden with pipes trundling past their homes as well as the dust and noise created on the site that drifted their way. The Queen would have her annus horribilis in 1992, but it came to Grange Lane 22 years earlier. The year had its downside for quite a few others as well. Ted Heath's Tories booted the Labour party out of office, the Beatles split up and Rolls Royce teetered on the edge of bankruptcy. Our soccer team lost the World Cup in Mexico and Tony Jacklin failed to retain the Open golf title. The year began with 'Two little boys' by Rolf Harris as the nation's top selling single. Now that was the sort of bad news that should have warned us what other disasters the following 12 months were going to bring!

Below: The sign by the roadworks tells pedestrians to keep right and then we see a barrier placed strategically in that very place. Still, who in his right mind would go left and risk falling into the pit created by the earth mover? The British are besotted with erecting signs that serve little purpose. Further along this section of the Sheffield Road area development was one stating 'roadworks'. Well, we could see that for ourselves and did we really need to have yet another announcing 'danger'? Here, at the Union Street and Duke Street junction in February 1968, work was in progress on the realignment of the road. It was just one part of the changing face of Barnsley that gathered pace in the late 1960s and throughout the 1970s. Anyone leaving the town in the swinging 60s and returning a dozen or so years later would have difficulty in recognising the place as roads changed and the town centre was remodelled. Across the country councils and corporations tried to come to terms with the shifting demands of society and our towns altered their whole personae as the word 'modernisation' became the in thing. Super highways and motorways were extended and ugly concrete shopping malls swept away traditional shops and markets. Architecture was confined to boring, rectangular shapes and many of our towns lost their individuality and their souls. There should have been a sign erected to warn us of that.

Above: The workmen attempting to rectify the cable fault at the junction of Wood Street, Agnes Road, New Street and Princess Street on 21 March 1968 were probably fed up with local wags who made comments as they went past. Some whistled the Bernard Cribbins' song 'Hole in the ground', popular in 1962, while others asked if they had reached Sydney yet. Modern health and safety do-gooders would have a field day with this scene. One tiny lamp marks the spot where a pile of debris clutters the side of the road. The light from that humble object would hardly have been enough for a motorist to spot or for an unwary pedestrian making his way home at night. In those days, should someone stumble into the hole, it was a case of blaming his clumsiness. Now, it would be an excuse to reach for the phone and dial up one of those no win no fee firms that regularly advertises on daytime television, trying to win clients among the bone idle sitting on their sofas of an afternoon. There are no barriers in place to warn off passers-by and the workers have little regard for hard hats. Oh how the 21st century regulators would love to come across such a situation. A stop order would be issued and managers hauled over the coals for permitting such a dangerous situation to occur and the little men in suits would have won another victory for bureaucracy.

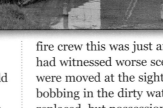

Below: Pity the poor folk living in the old people's bungalow at 50 Grange Lane on 13 April 1970. The fire brigade pumped thousands of gallons of River Dearne water from the garden and ground floor of this and other neighbouring properties. It would have been bad enough for anyone to endure, but for pensioners it seemed to be an even more cruel blow. Many of their treasured possessions were ruined, including personal keepsakes and mementoes of happy family life. Even after the floodwater was cleared there was the mud, silt and mess to be dealt with. Then there was that stench that lingered for months. Even when ruined carpets had been ditched and floors scrubbed, the odour persisted as it seemed to have pervaded the walls and lingered in every nook and cranny. Pity the poor souls who were not properly insured, being unable to afford the premiums. How could they hope to replace what had been lost? To the fire crew this was just another job, but even these men who had witnessed worse scenes in house fires and road crashes were moved at the sight of photographs of grandchildren bobbing in the dirty water. Chairs and televisions could be replaced, but possessions with sentimental attachments were different and heartbreaking for all concerned.

It's in the bag

Unknown to our ancestors, the thing about plastic is, well that it is quite literally plastic, capable of being made into any shape. This modern day wonder product has been very familiar to one Barnsley firm, which for almost half a century has been making polythene bags, puppets, gloves, containers for liquids, clothes covers and Christmas stockings.

Dale Products (Plastics) Ltd, today located on the Platts Common industrial estate, was founded in 1959 by Bernard Wilton Crawshaw.

Previously Bernard had had a varied career; he had designed and made bag machines for Darton Manufacturing, a packaging company which subsequently became BXL. Before then Bernard had worked for Slazenger Sports, designing machines for winding golf balls.

In 1959 Bernard left Darton Manufacturing to start up Dale Products, helped by his wife Marion and shortly after by Sid and Irene Cook.

Sid Cook was an engineer and worked for Dales as factory manager until retirement in the 1980s. Marion organised and ran the office, but often worked in the factory too. From that small start staff numbers would eventually reach almost 30.

A great innovator, Bernard would happily take on any work and worry about it later: with his engineering background he was adept at altering machines to do things their designers had never intended. One bagging machine designed by Bernard is still in use.

The business began in Station Road Worsborough, but five years later in 1964 it moved to Platts Common.

The factory was enlarged and extended up to the boundary in 1968 after a wooden store at the back of the factory was broken into by children who made a den under some of the plastic and lit candles with predictable results.

Bernard Crawshaw's son Michael joined the firm in 1980 from Polytechnic. He worked at first as an extruder operator then as a fitter. Bernard Crawshaw died in 1998, having already retired from the business. Today Michael Crawshaw is Managing Director, his mother Marion is Company Secretary.

*Above: Pictured at Dale Products 25th anniversary from left to right: Bernard Crawshaw, Marion Crawshaw, Irene Cook and Sid Cook. **Below left:** The production of policeman glove puppets. **Below:** Dale Products new Arvor bag machine, 2004.*

Coke: It's still the real thing

Since the advent of North Sea gas in the late 1960s there's been no mystery about where household gas comes from. But the younger generation may sometimes pause to wonder where we got our gas from before it was pumped to our homes from under the sea bed. What were those huge gasometers all about? Did you have to buy it in bottles? Was it distilled from crude oil?

Older readers of course know the secret. Take a lump of coal, heat it in the absence of air, and a miracle happens: the coal begins to give off gas. But there's more: valuable volatile oils are also given off, whilst the black tar within the coal begins to melt, dripping away to leave behind a crisp iron-grey honeycomb of coke - a honeycomb made of almost pure carbon - a smokeless fuel which burns at very high temperatures and without which the steel industry would never have existed.

Britain once boasted a great many coke plants. Today near Barnsley can be found one of only two remaining coke producers in the United Kingdom. The plant has been a familiar one to several generations of local folk, all of whom have indelible memories of the rich aroma of coal tar emanating from the site as well as equally indelible recollections of skies perpetually filled by rising clouds of steam.

The Monckton Coke & Chemical Company Ltd has been operating on the same site at Royston near Barnsley since the 1870s, producing high carbon content fuel and much more.

Founded using Lord Galway's family name in its official title ,what had been part of the Monckton Main Coal Company became the Monckton Coke & Chemical Company in 1920. The firm was acquired by ICI in 1964, and in 1994 by the predecessor of today's UK Coal.

Above: *Lord Galway.*
Below: *The Monckton Complex by night.*

received an English peerage in 1887 becoming Baron Monckton.

Baron Monckton's wife Vere would make her own contribution to the coke industry. In 1917 in the depths of the Great War Lady Monckton ran a munitions factory in Scarborough. Ammonia, a by product from the distillation of coal at the family owned works, was used in the manufacture of explosives. Munitions were an obvious, and it is to be presumed lucrative, expansion of the family enterprise. Vere, Lady Monckton died in 1921.

The Monckton name is in fact a direct reminder of George Edward Arundell-Monckton the sixth Viscount Galway who was born in 1805. The Monckton family could trace its origins to the 14th century and as soldiers, courtiers an statesmen would make their mark on the political map of Britain over a two hundred year period. As for local history the Monckton family and their pits would provide a lifetime's employment for thousands of local folk whilst also attracting an immigrant workforce from many other parts of the country to the area.

Until the mid 16th century coal gathered from outcrops had been free to anyone, but then a system of leasing coal from landowners, or renting land to be mined, began to be introduced. By the middle of the 17th century the Moncktons at Hodroyd were leasing land for this purpose to villagers.

In 1847 George Arundell-Monckton became MP for East Retford. Viscount Galway's greatest claim to fame however must be that in 1872 he established Hodroyd Colliery, and in 1874 Monckton Main.

The seventh Lord Galway, George Edmund Milnes Monckton, born in 1844, was Chairman of the Monckton group of companies for 55 years up until his death in 1931. He too became an MP and from 1872 to 1885 represented North Notts. until he

The title Baron Monckton became extinct in 1971 following the death without issue of Simon George Robert Monckton.

Full scale coke production began in 1878 soon after Monckton Main had begun full production. The mine was producing large quantities of slack or smudge in addition to solid lumps of saleable coal. The smudge had a very limited market and was being piled up in heaps. Charcoal had been the fuel used for centuries in the iron industry, but coke was an attractive alternative. Monckton's Board of Directors considered the possibility of converting their smudge into coke, and decided to build a new plant comprising no fewer than 12 coke ovens and a crushing machine.

Top: *An oven being charged with coal.*
Right: *Coke discharging through the guide into the Coke Car.*

By 1879 all 12 ovens had been completed at a cost of £360 and three were ready to begin production. Two years later another 12 ovens were in full production. By the end of 1881 42 ovens had been completed with even more planned.

Coke of course was not the only potential product from the coke making process and the opportunity to take advantage of chemical by-products was taken in 1884 when a further ten ovens were dedicated to extracting chemical by-products. In July that year 306 gallons of oil had been made from the ovens in one week. The total number of ovens now in use had reached 63 with 17 more planned.

By 1885 a gas plant was under construction, with plans to supply Royston with piped household gas: the job of laying mains pipes to Royston was soon in hand

The name Monckton Coke and Chemical Company was adopted in 1920. In 1947, as a subsidiary rather than an an asset of New Monckton Collieries Ltd, the coke plant was exempt from Nationalisation and; as a consequence rather than passing into state ownership the plant now came under the control of Monckton Holdings Ltd. A continuous programme of modernisa-

tion would take place over the following years under Monckton Holdings and continue after the company was bought by ICI in the 1960s and later under RJB Mining , subsequently UK Coal, which would run the plant alongside its coal mines formerly run by British Coal.

Today Monckton carbonises 300,000 tonnes of coal annually to produce 200,000 tonnes of coke from 42 Woodhall-Duckham gas ovens operating at temperatures of up to 1,295 degrees Celsius. The coke produced provides a carbon source for many industries, including kiln operators, sugar producers,

Top: An oven discharge by night.
Above: Trisomat Coke Screen.

All Monckton's activities are firmly based on safety, quality, flexibility and dependability. The company prides itself on being forward thinking and innovative, pursuing diversification through development of its plant, equipment and staff to meet future challenges and to grasp new opportunities. Not the least measure of Monckton's progress down the years has been the company's continuous improvements in compliance with the Integrated Pollution, Prevention and Control Regulations, a commitment which has done so much to improve the environment in recent decades.

Despite the demise of other coke works across the country Monckton not only continues to survive but to thrive. With 100 employees and an annual turnover of around £20 million, and a market with an insatiable appetite for coke, the company looks set to keep reminding us of its long heritage far into the new millennium.

Top left: The Charge Car being loaded beneath the 500 tonne Service Bunker. **Below:** *The Monckton Coke & Chemical site pictured in 2003.*

steel smelters, brick works and a fuel for the domestic market. Coke is also exported, mainly to the Scandinavian Ferro-Alloy and Ferro-Silica industries.

The coal used comes from Maltby Colliery. The mine works only one seam - Parkgate. The coal is low in both ash and phosphorous, which produces a consistently high quality coke with typically between 5 and six per cent ash and a tiny residue of phosphorous.

Gas is produced at an annual rate of some 100 million cubic metres. This is treated in the By-products plant, which also produces 14,500 tonnes of tar for the UK and European pitch markets; 3,000 tonnes of benzole is also produced for further refining in Europe to produce many other products, including benzene, toluene, xylene, styrene and naphthalene. A 20 per cent ammonia solution is also produced at the rate of around 4,000 tonnes annually.

Some 40 million cubic metres of the gas are used as an energy source for the carbonisation process, whilst the remaining 60 million cubic metres are used to raise high pressure steam in a Combined Heat and Power plant (CHP). Some of the steam, at a reduced pressure, is for site use; the rest is used in a turbine to produce electricity for use on site, and for export to the National Grid.

Potter magic

One of the oldest professions in the world is that of builder. Almost as soon as man stopped being a hunter gatherer he seems to have been unable to resist the temptation to pile one stone on top of another. And with building came civilisation; the very word being derived from 'town' - a town which someone had to build.

Individual builders come and go, but their works live on: some like the pyramids live on almost forever, a permanent reminder of those who worked on them.

The building industry however, is a volatile one. When demand for property is high building firms spring up like mushrooms - only to disappear again when market conditions decline; very few survive for long.

Top left: *Founder, Charles Dalton Potter.*
Below and right: *Early company vehicles.*

Barnsley's CD Potter & Son Ltd, builders and contractors, is however, the exception.

The original CD (Charles Dalton) Potter was born in Fishlake in 1858. Prior to 1907 he was already in business as a builder, working in partnership with a distant relative, John Potter, and a cousin Tom Potter.

The partnership of John, Tom and Charles Potter bought land and built homes. Dalton Terrace off Cemetery Road is named after CD Potter, Dalton being a family name.

Brian Panks joined the business in 1955 and became Managing Director in the late 1980s following Ralph Potter's death. Ralph would be the last Potter to have direct involvement with the firm.

During his years with Potters, Brian observed many changes in the business. At the beginning there was a lot of speculative building of pubs, schools, factories and houses. From the mid-1970s the emphasis switched to subsidence work for British Coal. That work carried on until the early 1990s when the firm began to concentrate on repairs, maintenance and one-off building projects.

In 1907 the partnership was dissolved and Charles Potter began trading on his own until his two sons Henry and Richard were old enough to join him.

Today the company's offices are still in an impressive Victorian building, not far from Dalton Terrace, and unpretentiously named 121 Doncaster Road where the business has now been based for almost a century. Once known by the grander title of Rhodes Villa, the office and its outbuildings were bought by Charles Potter's wife Anne in 1908.

Anne Reasbeck Potter would be commemorated by Potters when they built Reasbeck Terrace, off Wakefield Road. Charles Potter and his two sons had entered into a formal partnership, trading as CD Potter & Sons, in 1926. On 30th June 1928 that partnership was incorporated as CD Potter & Sons Ltd.

In 1928 Harry Potter bought out his brother Richard's share of Rhodes Villa and became the sole owner of the property.

Harry Potter died in 1948 at the age of 58; his son Ralph F Potter was made Managing Director on his father's death. Born in 1920, Ralph Potter passed away in 1993 after heading the family firm for most of the 20th century.

Both Ralph and his son Ian would become well known in Barnsley, both of them being Directors of Barnsley Football Club. That footballing connection was given added and poignant emphasis in 1999 when the company was asked to build a memorial to those who died in the Hillsborough disaster on the 10th anniversary of the ill-fated Liverpool v Nottingham Forest match of 15th April 1989.

Today the Potter family, represented by Ralph's widow Mrs Joan Potter together with her brother-in-law Kenneth and son Ian, are still the main shareholders in the business though they no longer directly manage the company.

Brian Panks retired in 2004, at which time Chris Barrow and Trevor Roberts became joint Managing Directors bringing with them a renewed commitment to introduce IT, implementing the latest in Health and Safety Regulations and recruiting staff of the required calibre and qualifications.

Today the firm concentrates on refurbishment and maintenance work, with 95 per cent of its activities being within the private sector.

The company pride itself on quality and never advertises for work, with all its commissions gained through its reputation and repeat business.

As for the future, slow and steady expansion in step with market forces, remains the Potter's magic formula.

Top left: *The Hillsborough Memorial, and inset, Brian Panks, Managing Director of CD Potter & Sons, and Keith Addy, Sheffield Wednesday Club President, pictured after the Memorial Stone was lowered onto its plinth.* ***Below:*** *C.D Potter & Sons Ltd staff, 2004.*

The best in the business - by a mile

We all know where to buy a used car - but what about a used industrial loading shovel? It may not be local common Knowledge, but situated in the village of Blacker Hill, Barnsley is a mile long industrial site full to bursting with good working second-hand wheeled loading shovels and spare parts. This is the home of Warwick Ward (Machinery) Ltd, a company founded in 1970 by Sheffield born Warwick Ward.

Having left school at 16 Warwick worked for locally based Thomas W. Ward Ltd (no relation) for 15 years rising through the ranks to become the leading salesman in the used equipment division. It was at this point that Warwick made a life changing decision; foregoing the comfort and security of his job and with two infant sons at home, he decided his talents were not being maximised and that he could do better on his own.

In 1970, with no fixed premises, and wife Susan assisting from their home Warwick bought his first loading shovel; quickly sold it on and with the proceeds bought another. The pattern continued with more loaders of varying makes and models being bought and sold and so the business was born. In 1973 an opportunity arose to buy a sizeable yard in Canal Street, Barnsley and Warwick snapped it up.

Top left: Founder, Warwick Ward.
Above right: Mr Hildebrand of Kilnsey Lime Ltd receives his first loading shovel from Warwick Ward whilst he was area representative for Thos. W. Ward Ltd 1967.Right: Warwick Ward's Blacker Hill site when first purchased, circa 1980, with Barrow Colliery in the background.

Warwick employed just two fitters at the yard; he could not have imagined his small company would grow to be the largest stockist of used loading shovels in the whole of Europe, employing over 30 full time staff, occupying a site more than five times larger and be exporting equipment to all four corners of the world.

Warwick readily admitted that he enjoyed buying the machines more than selling and it was this passion for buying loaders that led to the Canal Street yard to quickly fill with a huge array of plant. Using his hard earned knowledge and with his eye for a bargain he did not buy poor stock, only the best he could find. With the business expanding more than he ever imagined in 1978 Warwick invited his brother, Trevor to join him. Warwick saw the potential in stripping down the machines for which a buyer could not be found and selling the

By now the company was becoming world renowned for offering top quality used equipment with a service and value that was hard to match. A particular attraction for customers was the knowledge that if they bought a machine from Warwick Ward then if parts later wore out they could always get a replacement from the same company.

As the 1990's drew to a close, Warwick decided to gradually take a back seat and let the new generation move the business on. Sadly for all who ever had the good fortune to know him, Warwick lost a battle with brain cancer in January of 2004 but he was proud to know that the company that he created is still thriving and growing as Ashley and Matthew Ward, together with Trevor, aim to both maintain and improve the company's position in the 21st century. And they are well placed to do so.

good parts on, thereby setting up a spares division. Trevor, together with Barnsley born Richard Allen developed this part of the business, a division that would become a major part of the organisation.

As the years went by many older machines, though still working well, became obsolete with spare parts becomig impossible to obtain, Warwick Ward now developed the business by refurbishing many spare parts, enabling customers to buy reconditioned transmissions, axles and other components at a fraction of the cost of new ones and adding more years of valuable working life to plant which would otherwise have to be replaced

By 1980 the business once again had outgrown its home and the company moved to the present 15-acre site at Blacker Hill. The new site quickly filled, with one part of the yard full of working loading shovels and the other part being used for dismantling all types of machines.

In the mid 1980s, a new chapter in tbe company began when Warwick's two sons Matthew and Ashley joined the business. Matthew left school at 16 in 1984 and from the shop floor worked his way through the ranks. Ashley studied business and commerce at University and joined the company in 1987. Under the initial guidance of their father, both soon began to find their own niches and further expand the company. Matthew found that he was drawn naturally towards the buying side of the business whilst Ashley hugely enjoyed the challenge of finding a suitable home for the hundreds of machines that were purchased year on year.

For the future Warwick Ward's two sons are determined to run the company by the principles laid down by their father: good value for money and a personal service - always the mainstays of a family business - even one that has grown to global proportions but is still proud of its Yorkshire roots.

Top left: *The company's original Canal Street site.*
Top left inset: *One example of the hundreds of loading shovels available from Warwick Ward (Machinery) Ltd.*
Below: *'Miles Better', Warwick Wards mile long industrial site, Blacker Hill, Barnsley.*

From pop bottles to fire fighting
Walter Frank & Sons Ltd

In 1872 Hiram Codd invented the once-familiar soft drinks bottle sealed by an internal glass marble; although it was a great success production methods were initially slow and costly.

Walter Frank, a mould maker in the glass industry, invented a low cost method of producing these bottles. In 1881, with the money he received for his invention, Walter started his own business in a small shed behind his house in Mapplewell.

The business moved to its present site on Wakefield Road, Barnsley in 1910 and there, joined by his three sons, Walter built up a reputation for making high quality moulds for the production of glass bottles.

After Walter's death the company continued under the management of his son Donald, diversifying into the precision machining of components for electric generators during the second world war.

In 1947 Donald's nephews, Reginald, Kenneth and Brian Frank, joined their uncle, bringing with them further scientific

Top: *Kenneth Frank exhibits fire brigade equipment at Barnsley Civic Hall, 1965, attended by Mayor and Mayoress Mr and Mrs Butler and Chief Fire Officer Fred Hall.*
Below: *Staff pictured in the 1950s.* **Bottom right:** *From Left to right: Wilfred Kent, Jack Shone, Sam Kent (Wilfred's father) and Jim Strange pictured in front of a Lancashire Boiler, one of many converted into oil storage tanks during the second world war by Downings Construction Ltd.*

and engineering know-how. This allied to the company's existing expertise in precision machining, foundry work and mould-making produced a combination of engineering experience and skills which made possible the successful development of the aluminium alloy fire brigade equipment for which the company is now best known.

Until the 1940s fire brigade equipment, such as hose couplings and nozzles, were made of gunmetal and were very heavy. Attempts to lighten the equipment by using aluminium alloys failed initially because they were either too weak or too corrodable. Encouraged by Barnsley's Chief Fire Officers, TH Rumsey BEM and FR Hall MBE, QFSM, and assisted by Northern Aluminium Ltd, Walter Frank & Sons studied the aluminium alloys developed during the war and pioneered the use of the alloy now used, which is strong, corrosion resistant, and only one third the weight of gunmetal.

Initially aluminium castings were made elsewhere, from dies produced at Franks; but the advantages of making one's own castings soon became apparent and an aluminium foundry was started. The company now undertakes all stages of manufacture, from die making, casting, machining and assembly to final polishing, all on the same premises.

After the death of Donald Frank in 1969 his nephews Kenneth and Reginald ran the company until 1978 when they sold it to another Barnsley family firm, Downings Construction Ltd, which subsequently ceased its construction activities and was renamed Wilfred Kent Ltd.

Speed is all important in fire fighting, and any saving of weight in the equipment used can literally make the difference between life and death. The great advantage of Frank's light alloy equipment quickly became obvious in brigade competitions; its popularity spread so that today it is used not only throughout Britain but throughout the world.

From its earliest days Walter Frank has enjoyed a reputation for first class quality and in 1986 became the first company to be registered to BS 5750 for the manufacture of fire hose fittings. The range of fire brigade equipment such as standpipes, nozzles and hose couplings, is now the widest in the United Kingdom.

Although best known for its light alloy brigade equipment, the company diversified into fixed installation fire protection with the launch in 1992 of a new range of gunmetal fire hydrant valves.

In addition to its own range of products the company also produces cast non-ferrous components for several other manufacturers. A major development was the signing in 1998 of a Supplier Partnership agreement with world leaders Emco Wheaton, to supply raw castings for their range of petroleum road tanker valves. In order to meet price competition generally, and increase foundry output to service the Supplier Partnership agreement, a major investment programme was undertaken. Additional workshop space was created. A second CNC machining centre was installed and a new gravity diecasting facility added. The new plant was officially opened by local MP Eric Illsley.

Since the year 2000 Walter Frank has participated in a number of European research projects. Working with partners from throughout Europe the company has shared its expertise and, in return, gained the

knowledge and experience necessary to maintain the competitiveness of its tooling design and manufacture and foundry processes.

Product development continues, quality standard ISO 9001:2000 has been achieved and e-manufacturing is being introduced.

Today, under Chairman Wilfred Kent and his son Peter as Managing Director, Walter Frank & Sons Ltd has certainly come an awful long way from that day in 1881 when Walter Frank first set up his Barnsley business to make pop bottle moulds.

Top left: Team Leader, Darren Asquith, *demonstrates the new automatic diecasting machines.* ***Above:*** *From left to right: Roger Burnett (Emco Wheaton), Eric Illsley (MP), Peter Kent (Managing Director) and Wilfred Kent (Chairman) at the official opening of the new foundry facility in December 1998.* ***Below:*** *Graham Dewberry demonstrates the new universal machining centre.*

Fill that gap

Though we may not often spare it much thought a great deal of our modern world would quickly grind to a halt were it not for the efforts of companies like Barnsley's Seals Packings and Gaskets Ltd. The firm's products are used to seal against various fluids and gases. Additionally the company has expanded into heat insulation products in recent years.

In September 1971 the company was founded by Harry Harrison. Harry was a Cumbrian who had arrived in South Yorkshire in 1946 after spending six years in the Royal Artillery during the war.

Until 1971 Harry worked for a Sheffield company making seals and gaskets, but after being made redundant he decided to start his own business.

To start with the business made rubber and asbestos-based joints and gaskets with around four employees, a far cry from the 65 employed today.

Amongst the difficulties encountered in the early years was overcoming entrenched older established companies, whose products were firmly established in the minds of potential buyers. Perseverance and quality however paid off.

From 1971 until 1978 the business was based in Sheffield's Cadman Street until it relocated to Ecclesfield there it remained for three years until moving to Shaw Lane, Barnsley in 1981.

During the occupation of the Shaw Lane factory, previously owned by Beckets Mineral Water manufac-

turers, a spring was discovered under the property. The company was subsequently approached by a firm named Sheldale Developments with a view to selling the factory to them. Sheldale wanted to commercially exploit the spring water to meet the growing public appetite for bottled water.

By then the Shaw Lane factory had already been extended three times as the company needed more space. With no further space for expansion the Sheldale offer occurred at the best possible moment.

The current premises in the Mount Osborne Industrial Park were occupied in 1997, a move much helped by money raised from the sale of the Shaw Lane factory and its valuable spring water.

Today the company is still a family business. The founder's son, Jim Harrison, started as sales office junior before eventually becoming chairman.

Below left: *Cutting to size insulation boards.*
Below: *Replacement of seals supplied by SPG.*

when raw material costs have increased. Financial stability has been maintained through efficiency improvements.

But it has not only been increased efficiency which has been the key to progress. Quality and speed of service have also played their part, with deliveries made every day to some customers - direct to the production line if necessary. It's all part of SPG's 'Full Circle Solutions' concept which has transformed the business in its customers' eyes from merely being a commodity supplier into a partner capable of eliminating supply chain worries.

It also helps that staff know their business: all external sales staff, including Managing Director Simon Noble, are trained engineers.

Inevitably there has been a movement away from asbestos-based to asbestos-free jointing materials. On the sealing front SPG holds a distributor-ship for the Flexitallic range of semi-metallic gaskets, together with pump and valve gland packings also supplied by Flexitallic.

Gordon Adams joined the company shortly after its founding to run a busy internal sales office before eventually becoming Managing Director on Harry Harrison's retirement.

Another 'old hand' is Mike Wilkinson who joined the company in January 1973 to develop external sales, eventually becoming Sales and Technical Director.

In the firm's early days base materials were mainly sheet rubber, neoprene and asbestos-based jointing which were cut into bespoke joints and gaskets using wood form cutters and hydraulically operated Samco presses.

Original prices of raw materials were in the region of 2/- per lb. Currently materials costs anything between £8 and £100 per square metre. Modern CNC cutters and water jet cutters are now used as well as traditional presses.

Today SPG's main customers are found in the domestic heating equipment, power generation, electrical supply and general engineering industries.

The business has become increasingly competitive over the years; there has been little opportunity for price increases even

For the future it is intended to expand further, offering a wider range of services to petro-chemical and domestic heating manufacturing companies. An increased service in waterjet cutting operations will also be offered. Additionally the company has developed new insulation products, particularly for combustion chambers in domestic central heating boilers, converting high temperature fibre materials into bespoke shapes.

Top left: SPG's Waterjet cutting machine.
Above left: Thermal insulation fabrics which can be sewn to make fire blankets, welding curtains, bellows, tadpole tapes and seals. Below: SPG's premises, Mount Osborne Industrial Park, Barnsley.

Foundations of stone

Looking for a new garden shed? Need a ton of sand or a bag of gravel? Barnsley folk looking for building supplies don't have to look further than Hills Building Supplies Ltd based at 18 Carlton Road.

Though the present company name is not a particularly old the Hill name is one which has been familiar to the local building trade since just after the first world war.

Around 1920 a Barnsley miner, Joseph Hill, always known as Joe, bought a piece of land suitable for quarrying. In 1922 he added a horse and cart to his acquisition and set up a small business delivering stone out of his quarry to local builders.

On the face of it this period was a remarkably auspicious time to be setting up a small business. The end of the war in 1918 had seen a million servicemen discharged from the forces each one of them keen to begin constructing a world fit for heroes.

A post war economic boom saw new houses being built and new roads constructed. After years of horror and deprivation the good times seemed to have at last arrived.

Sadly such optimism was badly misplaced. The post war boom gradually faded away and unemployment soon began to rise and wages to fall, leading inevitably to industrial unrest. In 1929 came the Wall Street Crash which saw share prices plunge, and precipitated the great Depression of the 1930s. Many of those who had looked so wise setting out in business in the early 1920s now lost those businesses and found themselves jobless.

For Joe Hill however, the 1930s were not the disaster they were for so many others. Indeed in the 1930s the business became a little larger when Joe contracted to supply all the stone for the Rotherham Road. Any small improvement in personal prosperity however, had to be set against the gathering storm clouds over Europe. Herr Hitler had found his own way to bring Germany out of economic recession: rearmament.

For the construction industry the war which began in 1939 would be both a blessing and a curse. On the debit side was the shortage of men, as those young enough to fight were called up to the forces creating an instant shortage of labour. That labour shortage too would be reflected in the consequent shortage of supplies of all kinds.

Set against those problems was the surge in some kinds of building work which the war brought in its wake: the construction of aerodrome runways and air raid shelters, not to mention repairs to bomb damaged buildings.

Any real increase prosperity however had to wait until after the second world war when Joe's stone was in great demand for rebuilding.

By then Joe's sons Ned and Norman were old enough to do their share of the plentiful work. With Ned and Norman in the business a company was formed, Joseph Hill and Sons Ltd, which became the only company in the area to supply all types of aggregates. Harold Macmillan was by then

Top left: *Founder, Joe Hill.*
Left: *Ned and Edna Hill on a day trip in the 1960s.*

Prime Minister; 'You've never had it so good' he famously announced at an election rally. How right he was. Doomsayers had predicted that the 1950s would be a rerun on the 1920s - a brief post war boom followed once more by economic collapse and a return to the conditions of the hungry thirties. Happily in fact the decade saw an unprecedented level of growth, not least in the demand for building materials.

By the late 1950s Joe was ready for retirement and it would be left to the next generation to take the business forward into the next decade.

The two sons continued the business between them until 1964 when Ned left the old firm and, together with his wife Edna, formed the Hills South Yorkshire Agencies, a business which also supplied aggregates to the building trade.

In 1975 Ned Hill bought back Joseph Hill and Sons Ltd, turning it into a builders' merchants, whilst still retaining his aggregates business which by this time was also supplying the concrete industry.

Ned retired in the early 1990s leaving the business in the hands of his son, and Joe Hill's grandson, Steven Hill.

Above: An early Hills tipper truck, 1968.
Below: Hills Building Supplies, Carlton Road, Barnsley.

Lessons in History

Today Northern College has one of the most beautiful and impressive settings in the north of England. It is located at Wentworth Castle, Stainborough, just over three miles from the centre of Barnsley. Most of the buildings and surrounding park were designed during the 18th century. The main house is a Grade 1 listed building of outstanding historical importance, and it is surrounded by the only Grade 1 listed landscape in South Yorkshire. As well as being experienced as an educational establishment many folk today are also familiar with the buildings and grounds as an impressive setting for conferences and seminars, banquets and wedding receptions.

The 38 acres of grounds and gardens are of outstanding botanical and environmental interest. The gardens contain many varieties of rhododendron, camellia, magnolia and other Asiatic flowering plants as well as European species; in May and June each year the dazzling display of blooms attract many visitors. Together with the surrounding park and woodland they provide an important habitat for birds, insects, small mammals, fungi and wild flowers.

Top: *The baroque front of Wentworth Castle built by Thomas Wentworth, 1st Earl of Strafford.*
Bottom: *The spectacular entrance front of Wentworth-Woodhouse named after the medieval lords of Wentworth, photograph by John Flitcroft.*

It was in the 1940s that Wentworth Castle, until then a private home, was sold for future use as an educational establishment.

Wentworth Castle is a name that requires some explanation, not least since the building is not a castle but a country house and which stands, not at Wentworth, but at Stainborough. Until around 1730 the house was known as Stainborough Hall but was then renamed by Sir Thomas Wentworth the first Earl of Strafford who had recently enlarged the house and who had built a mock medieval castle on the site of an older earthwork on the highest point of his estate at Stainborough Low. That earthwork was the 'stone burgh' which had given Stainborough its name - 'low' being a word derived from the Old English word 'hlaw' meaning a hill.

The main entrance to the College is through the courtyard and the front door of the Cutler House built by Sir Gervase Cutler II in the late 17th century.

In the 20th century the owners of many country houses found it difficult to maintain their properties and were forced to sell them.

In 1948 Captain Vernon Wentworth sold the buildings and 60 acres of garden and park to Barnsley Education Committee for £26,000.

Death watch beetle, dry rot and the effects of military occupation during the second world war necessitated considerable expense, but the work was completed the following year when a teachers' training college for women specialising in nursery and primary school training was opened. Around the same time Wentworth Woodhouse was also turned into a teachers' training college creating some confusion in the public's mind.

In the 1960s Wentworth Castle shared in the national expansion of educational facilities and two modern teaching blocks were built, but the period of growth was short-lived, eventually leading to closure.

The building gained a new lease of life however when in 1978 it was converted to meet modern residential and safety standards and re-opened as the Northern College for Residential Adult Education.

The College acquired Home Farm in 1984; by 1986 the stable blocks had been converted into study bedrooms whilst car parks, tennis courts and sports pitches also enhanced the facilities available to students.

Despite such expansion Northern College happily remains a relatively small institution by contemporary standards; even so there are over 5,000 student registrataions each year. People come from many different backgrounds. They are men and women of all ages from 20 to over 70, often with families and dependants, some single parents accompanied by young or school age children, many familiar with unemployment or part time low paid jobs. What they have in common however, is their determination to secure the education, qualifications and opportunities they have previously been denied. They wish to take control of their lives and change them for the better. Many hope that by doing so that they can also improve the lives of those around them by being more effective citizens,

The College has pioneered an innovative mix of full and part time programmes of study which offer accredited pathways starting from basic literacy and numeracy through to higher education, not least with Diploma programmes which include humanities, trade union studies, computing and community regeneration.

Top: The Cutler House, built by Sir Gervase Cutler II circa 1672 which is now the home of the Northern College. Centre: A montage of courses provided by Northern College for Residential Adult Learning.

Acknowledgments

The publishers would like to thank

Local Studies, Barnsley Central Library,

Andrew Mitchell

Steve Ainsworth

Memories of Accrington - 1 903204 05 4

Memories of Barnet - 1 903204 16 X

Memories of Barnsley - 1 900463 11 3

Golden Years of Barnsley -1 900463 87 3

Memories of Basingstoke - 1 903204 26 7

Memories of Bedford - 1 900463 83 0

More Memories of Bedford - 1 903204 33 X

Golden Years of Birmingham - 1 900463 04 0

Birmingham Memories - 1 903204 45 3

Memories of Blackburn - 1 900463 40 7

More Memories of Blackburn - 1 900463 96 2

Memories of Blackpool - 1 900463 21 0

Memories of Bolton - 1 900463 45 8

More Memories of Bolton - 1 900463 13 X

Bolton Memories - 1 903204 37 2

Memories of Bournemouth -1 900463 44 X

Memories of Bradford - 1 900463 00 8

More Memories of Bradford - 1 900463 16 4

More Memories of Bradford II - 1 900463 63 6

Bradford Memories - 1 903204 47 X

Bradford City Memories - 1 900463 57 1

Memories of Bristol - 1 900463 78 4

More Memories of Bristol - 1 903204 43 7

Memories of Bromley - 1 903204 21 6

Memories of Burnley - 1 900463 95 4

Golden Years of Burnley - 1 900463 67 9

Memories of Bury - 1 900463 90 3

More Memories of Bury - 1 903 204 78 X

Memories of Cambridge - 1 900463 88 1

Memories of Cardiff - 1 900463 14 8

More Memories of Cardiff - 1 903204 73 9

Memories of Carlisle - 1 900463 38 5

Memories of Chelmsford - 1 903204 29 1

Memories of Cheltenham - 1 903204 17 8

Memories of Chester - 1 900463 46 6

More Memories of Chester -1 903204 02 X

Memories of Chesterfield -1 900463 61 X

More Memories of Chesterfield - 1 903204 28 3

Memories of Colchester - 1 900463 74 1

Nostalgic Coventry - 1 900463 58 X

Coventry Memories - 1 903204 38 0

Memories of Croydon - 1 900463 19 9

More Memories of Croydon - 1 903204 35 6

Golden Years of Darlington - 1 900463 72 5

Nostalgic Darlington - 1 900463 31 8

Darlington Memories - 1 903204 46 1

Memories of Derby - 1 900463 37 7

More Memories of Derby - 1 903204 20 8

Memories of Dewsbury & Batley - 1 900463 80 6

Memories of Doncaster - 1 900463 36 9

More Memories of Doncaster - 1 903204 75 5

Nostalgic Dudley - 1 900463 03 2

Golden Years of Dudley - 1 903204 60 7

Memories of Edinburgh - 1 900463 33 4

More memories of Edinburgh - 1903204 72 0

Memories of Enfield - 1 903204 14 3

Memories of Exeter - 1 900463 94 6

Memories of Glasgow - 1 900463 68 7

More Memories of Glasgow - 1 903204 44 5

Memories of Gloucester - 1 903204 04 6

Memories of Grimsby - 1 900463 97 0

More Memories of Grimsby - 1 903204 36 4

Memories of Guildford - 1 903204 22 4

Memories of Halifax - 1 900463 05 9

More Memories of Halifax - 1 900463 06 7

Golden Years of Halifax - 1 900463 62 8

Nostalgic Halifax - 1 903204 30 5

Memories of Harrogate - 1 903204 01 1

Memories of Hartlepool - 1 900463 42 3

Memories of High Wycombe - 1 900463 84 9

Memories of Huddersfield - 1 900463 15 6

More Memories of Huddersfield - 1 900463 26 1

Golden Years of Huddersfield - 1 900463 77 6

Nostalgic Huddersfield - 1 903204 19 4

Huddersfield Town FC - 1 900463 51 2

Memories of Hull - 1 900463 86 5

More Memories of Hull - 1 903204 06 2

Hull Memories - 1 903204 70 4

Memories of Ipswich - 1 900463 09 1

More Memories of Ipswich - 1 903204 52 6

Memories of Keighley - 1 900463 01 6

True North Books Ltd - Book List

Memories of Kingston - 1 903204 24 0

Memories of Leeds - 1 900463 75 X

More Memories of Leeds - 1 900463 12 1

Golden Years of Leeds - 1 903204 07 0

Memories of Leicester - 1 900463 08 3

Leeds Memories - 1 903204 62 3

More Memories of Leicester - 1 903204 08 9

Memories of Leigh - 1 903204 27 5

Memories of Lincoln - 1 900463 43 1

Memories of Liverpool - 1 900463 07 5

More Memories of Liverpool - 1 903204 09 7

Liverpool Memories - 1 903204 53 4

Memories of Luton - 1 900463 93 8

Memories of Macclesfield - 1 900463 28 8

Memories of Manchester - 1 900463 27 X

More Memories of Manchester - 1 903204 03 8

Manchester Memories - 1 903204 54 2

Memories of Middlesbrough - 1 900463 56 3

More Memories of Middlesbrough - 1 903204 42 9

Memories of Newbury - 1 900463 79 2

Memories of Newcastle - 1 900463 81 4

More Memories of Newcastle - 1 903204 10 0

Newcastle Memories - 1.903204 71 2

Memories of Newport - 1 900463 59 8

Memories of Northampton - 1 900463 48 2

More Memories of Northampton - 1 903204 34 8

Memories of Norwich - 1 900463 73 3

Memories of Nottingham - 1 900463 91 1

More Memories of Nottingham - 1 903204 11 9

Nottingham Memories - 1 903204 63 1

Bygone Oldham - 1 900463 25 3

Memories of Oldham - 1 900463 76 8

Memories of Oxford - 1 900463 54 7

Memories of Peterborough - 1 900463 98 9

Golden Years of Poole - 1 900463 69 5

Memories of Portsmouth - 1 900463 39 3

More Memories of Portsmouth - 1 903204 51 8

Nostalgic Preston - 1 900463 50 4

More Memories of Preston - 1 900463 17 2

Preston Memories - 1 903204 41 0

Memories of Reading - 1 900463 49 0

Memories of Rochdale - 1 900463 60 1

More Memories of Reading - 1 903204 39 9

More Memories of Rochdale - 1 900463 22 9

Memories of Romford - 1 903204 40 2

Memories of Rothertham- 1903204 77 1

Memories of St Albans - 1 903204 23 2

Memories of St Helens - 1 900463 52 0

Memories of Sheffield - 1 900463 20 2

More Memories of Sheffield - 1 900463 32 6

Golden Years of Sheffield - 1 903204 13 5

Memories of Slough - 1 900 463 29 6

Golden Years of Solihull - 1 903204 55 0

Memories of Southampton - 1 900463 34 2

More Memories of Southampton - 1 903204 49 6

Memories of Stockport - 1 900463 55 5

More Memories of Stockport - 1 903204 18 6

Memories of Stockton - 1 900463 41 5

Memories of Stoke-on-Trent - 1 900463 47 4

More Memories of Stoke-on-Trent - 1 903204 12 7

Memories of Stourbridge - 1903204 31 3

Memories of Sunderland - 1 900463 71 7

More Memories of Sunderland - 1 903204 48 8

Memories of Swindon - 1 903204 00 3

Memories of Uxbridge - 1 900463 64 4

Memories of Wakefield - 1 900463 65 2

More Memories of Wakefield - 1 900463 89 X

Nostalgic Walsall - 1 900463 18 0

Golden Years of Walsall - 1 903204 56 9

More Memories of Warrington - 1 900463 02 4

Memories of Watford - 1 900463 24 5

Golden Years of West Bromwich - 1 900463 99 7

Memories of Wigan - 1 900463 85 7

Golden Years of Wigan - 1 900463 82 2

Nostalgic Wirral - 1 903204 15 1

Wirral Memories - 1 903204 747

Memories of Woking - 1 903204 32 1

Nostalgic Wolverhampton - 1 900463 53 9

Wolverhampton Memories - 1 903204 50 X

Memories of Worcester - 1 903204 25 9

Memories of Wrexham - 1 900463 23 7

Memories of York - 1 900463 66 0